LIFE IN AMANA

Reporters' Views
of the Communal Way, 1867–1935

Amana, a general view from The Communist Societies of the United States *by Charles Nordhoff, Harper and Brothers, 1875.*

Compiled by Joan Liffring-Zug Bourret
Edited by Dorothy Crum

Penfield
Press

Lithograph by Joseph Prestele, Sr., circa 1850
Joseph Prestele made this plate, drawn and engraved on stone,
after his arrival in America to join the Community of True Inspiration.

Assistant editors: Melinda Bradnan, Jacqueline Comito, Eric Heskje, Marlene Perrin, Lynn Ridenour, and Dwayne Bourret

Graphic design: Dana Lumby and Walter Meyer

For their assistance, we thank the staff of the Museum of Amana History and Mary Bennett, archivist, State Historical Society of Iowa.

Contributors making this publication possible include:

The Museum of Amana History
The Amana Society
Schanz Furniture and Refinishing and Broom and Basket Shop
Mike Simmons and Newspapers of Iowa County
Brick House and Red Fox Paper Den

Covers: Background of Inspirationist calico block print tablecloth, circa 1840s. Museum of Amana History collection.

Preface

By Lanny Haldy, Director, Amana Heritage Society

Although he is perhaps the best known, Charles Nordhoff was not the only—or even the first—newspaperman to visit the Community of True Inspiration in Amana, Iowa. In the period 1867–1924 we find reports, for example, by correspondents of the *Elmira, New York Telegram,* the *Somerville, Massachusetts Journal,* and the *Minneapolis Journal.* In Iowa, the *Des Moines Register* featured the Amana community several times, and the *Cedar Rapids Republican* regularly sent correspondents to cover events in the colony. The *Cedar Rapids Gazette* printed at least forty-two articles on Amana in its first twenty-five years of publication, beginning in 1883. Despite differences in time, geography, and degree of familiarity, these accounts reveal a remarkably similar view of communal Amana. Furthermore, the newspaper stories demonstrated that from an early date communal Amana was a popular new subject, not an isolated unknown, and provide many examples of how the community opened itself to outsiders.

Bertha Shambaugh's introduction to her 1908 study, *Amana the Community of True Inspiration,* presented an image of communal Amana and its attendant themes that are dominant in late nineteenth- and early twentieth-century accounts:

"In one of the garden spots of Iowa there is a charming little valley from which the surrounding hills recede like the steps of a Greek theater. Through this valley the historic Iowa River flows peacefully to the eastward. A closer view reveals seven old-fashioned villages nestling among the trees or sleeping on the hillsides. About these seven villages stretch twenty-six thousand goodly acres clothed with fields of corn, pastures, meadows, vineyards, and seas of waving grain. Beyond and above, surrounding the little valley, are richly timbered hills, forming, as though by design, a frame for this quaint picture of Amana—the home of the Community of True Inspiration.

"A bit of Europe in America, a voice out of the past on the world's western frontier, this unique community stands as the nearest approach in our day to the Utopian's dream of a community of men and women living together in peace, plenty, and happiness, away from the world and its many distractions. But the communism of Amana is not a dream: it is a fact—an established order of life."

Shambaugh's pastoral lines are well known and very often echoed by later writers on communal Amana up to the present day. Her image of Amana as an idyllic garden spot, quaint and old-fashioned, where the beauty and bounty of the landscape mirrors the lives of the residents living together in peace and plenty, has a powerful attraction that can lure the casual visitor as well as the most hard-nosed academician. Amana was an example of a communist system that is neither a fantastic dream nor abstract theory.

The essential features of the garden image that would become common in subsequent news stories, and be codified later by Shambaugh, were introduced in the first known extant newspaper account of Amana published in the Davenport, Iowa *Daily Gazette,* June 29, 1867. This article is the first "outside" account of Amana known to exist. The article was part of a series, neatly delineated in the headline: "Iowa as Is/Pen Sketches of Town and Country/The Towns of the C.R.I.&P. Railroad/The Amana Society."

In this series, the characterization of the Amana people was of a prosperous people in a garden spot. The people were sincere, virtuous, devout, and earnest. Their industrious nature was self-evident, but "it cannot be said that they work hard."

This view of Amana was of a successful and wealthy cooperative society where the richness of the land is reflected in the richness of life. Furthermore, the author was convinced that the wealth of Amana contributed to the growth and wealth of the state of Iowa. Forty years later some local and area newspapers would suggest that the converse was true—that the Amana community was an economic liability to the county and state.

The themes of garden, communist success, and wealth that appear in the Davenport *Daily Gazette* article surfaced again and again in newspaper accounts of the community in the late nineteenth and early twentieth centuries. Visitors to Amana from local papers, as well as from more distant cities, commonly used the same motifs, themes and words to describe the colony. And as time passed the idea of a successful, quaint garden spot in Iowa became more exaggerated. What was already a remarkable example of cooperative success in 1867 was even more noteworthy in 1923, and what was a quaint and peculiar community on the Iowa frontier turned into a picturesque, if anachronistic, paradise in post-World War I America. For the popular press, the Amana Community was the land that time forgot.

As late as 1923, just a few years before the communal system was abandoned, the *Cedar Rapids Gazette* could still stretch a headline over the top of its second page that praised the endurance of the community: "Amanas—World's Only Successful Communistic Colony." The notion of a prosperous garden spot was still strong, as the subheadings demonstrate: "Social or Economic Reforms not Preached by the Society, Strife does not enter Lives," or "Big, Happy Family is way one member describes most novel community in United States." This happy state of affairs is all possible, of course, because the community of Amana is not that of social theorists, but rather based on religious principles and Christian faith.

The image of a garden paradise remains part of the popular notion of Amana's communal experience long after the reorganization of the economy of the Society in 1932. Although national and world politics led many popular writers to characterize Amana's "Great Change" as a triumph of capitalism over communism, still others could look back on communal Amana as a time of Utopian glory. For those writers, such as Marcus Bach in 1961, Amana's abandonment of the communal system was seen as the moment when "Utopia was absorbed by its arch enemy—the world."

Parts of this article are from In All the Papers: Newspaper Accounts of Communal Amana, 1867–1924, *by Lanny Haldy, originally published by the Communal Studies Association in the* Communal Societies Journal, Vol. XIV, 1994.

Introduction

*"Behold, thou art fair, my love...thou has
doves' eyes within thy locks...thy lips are like
a thread of scarlet, and thy speech is
comely...Thou art all fair, my love...Come
with me from Lebanon, my spouse, with me
from Lebanon: look from the top of
Amana..."*

— From Song of Solomon,
Chapter 4, Verses 1 – 8

By John Zug

The Amanas are a wispy brush of soft memory across the face of a yesterday that never can quite be recreated, even in the mind. For time changes relentlessly, and with it come changes in the faces and beliefs of the people, and even in the face of the earth as they place upon it their mark.

Here was the New World home of the Community of True Inspiration, founded in 1855 by a people who quit the Old World's persecution and ventured west seeking the opportunity to worship God in their own way.

Their way was communal—from each according to his abilities, to each according to his needs. There were 25,000 rich acres, and each member—of German, Swiss, and Alsatian ancestry—handed down his skills from father to son, from mother to daughter, in the Old World tradition. Thus were manned the farms, woolen mills, meat smoking plants, furniture factory, wineries, community kitchens, and other industries.

In 1932, by a vote of the people, the Amanas dropped the communal way and took the great step into the system of free enterprise that surrounded them. The Amanas today blend time-honored craftsmanship with 20th century efficiency.

But Amana offers more. In a peaceful setting from another age, the visitor finds scenic views, places of interest and museums—a nostalgic backward glance and a hopeful look into the future.

Contents

GREAT CHANGE AND CORPORATE LIFE

HISTORY

From *The History of the Amana Society* or

Community of True Inspiration

By William Rufus Perkins and Barthinius L. Wick,
University of Iowa, 1891.

A group of German Lutherans who were dissatisfied with the cold formalism of the clergy began to hold their own meetings in private homes in the latter half of the seventeenth century and were called Pietists. The founder of the sect was Philip Jacob Spener, an emigrant Lutheran divine. After Spener's death his followers founded new sects or joined other denominations. In one group, members prophesied like the prophets of old. They were called Inspirationists. Two with the particular gift of inspiration were Eberhard Ludwig Gruber (1665-1728) and Johann Friedrich Rock (1678-1749), considered the real founders of what would become the Amana Society.

It is around these two men, their "heroes of faith," that the development and progress of the community has turned as if on an axis. They were both from Wurtemberg. The former was a clergyman in the Lutheran church. He lost his position because he defended the doctrines of Spener, and because he tried to do away with the outward forms of religion. They are always magnified more when the spirit of true religion dies out. For this, Gruber had to withdraw from the church. Rock was a preacher's son, of a peculiar temperament and of a mystical cast of mind. He was a saddler by trade, but had received a good education. He read much about religion, but found no sect whose doctrines could satisfy his yearnings after truth. In Stuttgart he found a small body of serious believers presided over by a Dr. Hedinger. It was at one of Hedinger's meetings that Gruber and Rock met for the first time; an intimate friendship arose between them, which lasted for life.

Around Gruber and Rock the obscure and the illiterate assembled to hear explained and unfolded the principles of that spiritual kingdom which all sought to find. Patiently and assiduously Rock and Gruber labored to instruct their countrymen in divine things and in the knowledge of virtue. These men wanted to free the ignorant peasants from the heavy burdens imposed by the corrupt clergy, and to lead them to a purer and more exalted communication with God. To accomplish this end they toiled and suffered all sorts of persecution; firm in their belief they unostentatiously went into every nook and corner of Germany, penetrated into Switzerland, and visited many parts of France and Holland. The gentleness of their manners, the purity and simplicity of the doctrines they preached convinced many, but the hatred of the clergy, who looked with disgust on any change in the form of things, knew no bounds. The preachers were put in prison, they were fined and persecuted, but they were not silenced.

In 1720, the society organized with Gruber and Rock as presiding elders. Meetings were established in five German cities. Gruber died at age sixty-three in 1728, and Rock died at age seventy in 1749.

After the death of Rock, in 1749, Inspiration ceased. The society still had many eminent divines enlisted in its ranks, but they did not possess this remarkable gift.

Flourishing meetings were kept up in Ysenburg, Wittgenstein, Neuwied, Homburg, Switzerland, Elsass and Wurtemberg. The older men were passing away and the younger ones who took their places, although they may have had the ability, lacked the enthusiastic spirit of the older ones. They began more and more to lead a quiet life. They grew rich and fell back among the worldly. It had been prophesied that new men should arise to carry on the work taken up by Gruber and Rock, but years passed without any signs of the fulfillment of the prophecy.

The dawn finally came; the revival came, unnoticed and unheralded. It brought new blood and new life into the society, and from this time its future was to a certain extent assured. The first who began to prophesy, after this gift had ceased for over half a century, was Michael Kraussert of Strasburg. His gift was recognized and he began to travel and preach, again arousing the old enthusiasm. However, in a few years he fell back, and finally lost his power of prophecy.

Barbara Heinemann (1795-1883)

The most remarkable person, perhaps, who was ever connected with the society was Barbara Heinemann, a poor, ignorant peasant girl from Leuterville, Lower Elsass, where she was born in 1795. She was one of the first inspired in the revival, one who had experienced the oppression which the government practiced more and more towards the members of the society during their last years in Germany, and she followed the little flock to America in search of freedom and a home. She experienced all the trials to which they were exposed in the first settlement near Buffalo, New York. She was one of the first to come to Iowa, where she again took up her work, a work which did not cease until 1883, when she was laid to rest, without any outward show but with much inward feeling [by members of the society], in the Amana cemetery, at the advanced age of eighty-eight.

Her parents were pious people. They were in such poor circumstances that Barbara never attended school a day in her life, but at the early age of eight was sent to a neighboring factory, where she earned a little pittance at spinning wool. In 1813, a financial crisis occurred, caused by Napoleon's endless wars. After the battle of Leipzig the entire country suffered from panic. The factory in which Barbara had worked for ten years was closed and she was compelled to go out as a servant.

While she worked in the factory, she had been of a lively disposition; now a peculiar state of mind bordering on melancholy suddenly clouded her lively temperament. She gave up her work and returned home, in hope of improvement. She frequently attended church, for if she engaged constantly in prayer, she thought this gloom might pass away. Once, as she partook of the sacrament, the priest said, "Who is unworthy and drinks, he drinks judgment unto himself." This made a deep impression upon her mind, and she solemnly promised so to guide her life as to be acceptable to God.

She conversed with the priest and all of the godly mothers of the neighborhood regarding the state of her mind, but no one could explain it satisfactorily nor relieve her melancholy. One woman said she acted like the Pietists, of which people Barbara had never heard. She loved solitude and spent much of her time wandering about in the fields communing with God and nature. One night she had a dream telling her how her conversion was to take place. "I sat in a room at dusk," she says in her *Memoirs*, "contemplating the mercy of God; I saw my youthful companions without, joyful and happy, and anxious to have me join them; but I sat unmoved, not knowing whether to go or not, when I heard a loud voice, which penetrated marrow and bone, bidding me remain. I began to feel easier, and perceived that God had heard my prayers." Feeling uncomfortable on account of this dream, she proceeded to Sulz, where a few Pietists were said to live.

She was kindly received by these people who did all in their power to console and comfort her. She told her dream, which they believed would come true if she would only listen to God's voice when it was heard.

She remained with these people for several months, slowly improving in mind, when M. Kraussert came to the neighborhood on a religious visitation. Barbara was glad to find someone who took an interest in her depression of mind—someone who could explain to her all the trials she had passed through in the last few years. He thought that she would become inspired and speak at meetings. To become better acquainted with the Inspirationists and their doctrines, she accompanied M. Kraussert to Bergzabern, Bavaria. On Christmas Day 1818, at the age of twenty three, she became inspired for the first time in one of their meetings. Although she knew nothing from books, she spoke in the language of the schools, for it was fluent, clear and free from error. Kraussert became subject to Inspiration and affirmed all she had said, feeling, as he did, that it came from God.

She joined the society and went about doing religious work, but she was arrested, along with Mr. Kraussert and Christian Metz (1793-1867). All were accused of heresy by the city magistrate. They remained in prison only a short time, as nothing could be proved against them.

She became inspired at the meetings, in the fields, while at work, at home, or on journeys. For this reason persons always accompanied her to take down what she said while under this influence. These revelations are still read by members of the society for edification and consolation, and after a lapse of nearly a century, they have lost none of their flavor.

This state of mind caused jerkings and twitchings of the body for a short time before she began to speak, so that she was conscious of what was coming on. She could prophesy with great exactness what was likely to take place. When she concentrated her mind upon those things which she wished to know, it caused a nervous exhaustion from which she did not easily recover.

The persecutions Barbara Heinemann had to suffer at the hands of the magistrates were not all the trials she had to pass through. Members of the society who were rich and influential were not pleased to have the poor, ignorant peasant girl looked upon as prophetess and as a minister of the gospel. All sorts of accusations were brought against her. She patiently submitted to these wrongs, and she was, for a short period, expelled from the society. The accusations, which were false, were withdrawn; the few who had conspired against her were expelled, and she was reinstated to the comfort of the society and her own consolation.

The society was reorganized. Besides the twenty-one articles of E.L. Gruber, the twenty-four articles of Johann Adam Gruber (his son) were adopted as the basis of their faith. The members became more and more enthusiastic in the work; the society increased in numbers, and everything pointed to a brilliant future.

In 1823, Barbara Heinemann was married to George Landmann. Her gift of Inspiration had ceased, and did not return until 1849; from that time she continued to be inspired until the time of her death.

This woman was the only one in the society who possessed the gift of Inspiration after the death of Christian Metz in 1867, and since her death, no one has so far been able to take her place. She was a woman who possessed many noble qualities; meek and patient in suffering, she knew how to comfort those in trouble; how to touch a tender spot in the hearts of those who were wayward and lukewarm in matters of religion; always keeping her presence of mind, she could censure without offense and exhort without ranting; of an amiable disposition, she was respected and venerated by all who knew her.

All the education she received she acquired herself without the aid of a teacher, and when she learned how to read and write, her joy was great, for she felt an inward delight to be able to commune with God through the Holy Scriptures. Although she knew nothing of the philosophies of the schools, she could analyze the "common sense" philosophy of the heart. What she uttered during those periods when she was inspired seems the product of deep thought, coming from the serene depths of a soul that understood the highest and noblest motives in man.

Christian Metz (1793 - 1867)

Christian Metz, a son of Jacob Metz of Neuwied, previously mentioned, also became inspired about 1820. He was a man of much executive ability, and the temporal affairs of the society were nearly all conducted by him up to the time of his death in 1867.

The name Metz is of frequent occurrence in the history of the organization from the time of its foundation. Originally from Elsass, whence Johann George Metz was driven on account of his religious views in 1716, it is in Hessen that the family, for over a century, toiled and suffered for the principles which the founder held dearer than home or native land.

Christian Metz was not only an organizer; he was a preacher and writer as well. He made five visits to Switzerland; visited Elsass, Lorraine, Saxony, and Wurtemberg many times. In all these places, he won converts to his cause. In 1824, Metz was prominent in winning over many Herrnhutters,* who had estranged themselves from that body.

In Wurtemberg there lived a number of pious people called Michelians, named after the founder, Michel Hahn, a pious mystical preacher who had exercised much influence by his reformatory measures. After his death the believers were scattered, not knowing what denomination to join and too weak to continue the work their founder had begun. When Christian Metz happened to pass through the country on a religious visitation, a few of them joined the society. They did not long enjoy the peace and comfort they found within its protection, for the French government oppressed and persecuted all dissenters in Elsass and Strasbourg, and they were driven out of France and came as fugitives to Germany, where they found a home with their fellow believers in Hessen.

In 1833, Switzerland took steps toward Conservatism, caused by a relapse of the revolutionary spirit of 1830. Oaths had to be taken in

---

* A colony of Moravian Brethren founded by Graf von Zinzendorf, as was the community of Herrnhut in the Dresden district of Germany.

14

order to swear fealty to the government, and every able-bodied man at a certain age had to learn the art of war. Many families left their native land and came to Hessen. Two years later several more came; the most prominent of the newcomers were Scheuner, Trautmann, Moser, Benedict and Hieronimus Gasser, and Aeshlimann.

From Basal came Burgy, Graf, Landmann, Salathe, and Weckerling. Gottlieb Ackermann came from Lauenheim in Saxony. His family belonged to the Gichtelians, followers of a revivalist by the name of Gichtel.

With all these exiles thrown upon the society, without any means, and for the most part without work, the members were in great perplexity. Christian Metz, farsighted and thoughtful, came to the conclusion that the best method would be for the society to lease some large estate where the exiles could be put to work and make enough to supply their wants, the society paying the rent.

The Marienborn castle, between Bergheim and Ronneburg, which formerly had belonged to the Herrnhuters, was leased by the society. But this was not enough, for members kept coming from Wurtemberg, from Elsass, and from Switzerland; besides it was not well to have the different nationalities together, as their dialects and customs were different. By 1834, three more castles with adjoining estates were leased, one at Armenburg where the Swiss had found a home; another at Engelthal where the Wurtemberg exiles were placed; and still another at Haag.

For the use of these estates the society paid an annual sum of 18,000 florins. As high as five and one-half florins were paid for the use of a morgen (2.116 acres) of land.

The members lived, for the most part, together in the castle or adjoining buildings, and in a large room in the castle, meetings were held and the children were taught; they worked the land together, sold the products, and divided the proceeds equally. At first they did not eat at the same table, but when they saw that it would be cheaper to eat together, this plan was adopted.

Here we have the first beginnings of the communistic life, which the society afterwards adopted. It arose unconsciously, from small beginnings, with no thought of the results which would flow from it.

A few of the members were artisans and preferred to work at their old trades rather than work on the estates. Therefore the societies rented a few factories where those who were skilled in trades were placed. The members at the Castle of Haag leased a woolen mill, a grist mill, and an oil mill, the expenses being borne by the society, which was taxed to its utmost in order to satisfy all bills and to keep the wolf from the door. In Armenburg a woolen mill was erected by the society so that the members could find employment.

For a time it seemed impossible for the society to take care of all who came, but soon their woolen goods became famous throughout the country. They had adopted the motto, "Honesty is the best policy," a motto which they have always lived up to in all their dealings. The goods were more and more in demand. It was found that they used the best material and took the greatest care in the making of them.

In 1837, the first love feast since the revival of 1817 was held at Armenburg. Jacob Dorr of Bergheim and William Metz, a cousin of C. Metz, both joined the society in which they worked faithfully for the furtherance of their creed.

Many people belonging to other denominations came to visit the members of the society, having heard or read much about their peculiar ways.

There had been a contest fought in the courts years before as to whether an affirmation could be made instead of an oath, and whether persons conscientiously could learn the art of war when their lives and their principles were those of peace. Some principalities had decided in favor of the society, others against it. Hesse-Darmstadt had been the most liberal, and it was in this principality that the majority of them found a refuge. But enemies who were jealous of the success of the society soon began to stir up a feeling of dissatisfaction among the ruling classes, and so the old liberties were little by little taken away.

When the year 1841 had arrived, things had come to a crisis, for encroachments had been made from all sides. The members assembled quietly and drew up a last imploring request to the ministry at Darmstadt, begging for more freedom. They wished to affirm instead of taking an oath in civil matters, claiming that it was inconsistent with the Scriptures to take an oath. They wished to educate their own children and were willing to support the state schools besides. Up to this time the children had been obliged to attend the other schools, where instruction was nearly all of a character in accordance with the established church. They said they could not take up arms, believing it to be inconsistent with the Bible; therefore, they could not conscientiously spend the best years of their lives in learning the art of war, which seemed so inconsistent with true religion.

It was decided that none of these requests could be granted. This decision seemed the death-knell to the very existence of the society, for faithful believers had come as exiles and fugitives from many parts of Europe, and now their hope of toleration was destroyed.

But great changes had taken place in Europe from 1830 to 1840. When the French for a third time discarded their king, altered their constitution and chose a "citizen king" for ruler, the elements of discontent were set in motion all over Europe. Kings trembled, and ministers, narrow and superstitious, advised the rulers to press the yoke more firmly on the people so that they would not rebel.

Revolts broke out in nearly every large city in Europe. The Poles rose in an unsuccessful attempt to throw off their shackles; the Belgians proclaimed their independence; while in Italy, Mazzini, the patriot and prophet of Italian liberty, arose from obscurity; in England, the Reform Bill, the slavery agitation and Chartism were convulsing the public mind; but Germany, always conservative, rather fell back a step than took a stride forward in the march of freedom and reform.

Besides the unfortunate results which had directly or indirectly come from this revolutionary spirit which had spread discontent among some nations and freedom among others, there were other causes which led to dissatisfaction and finally removal upon the part of the Society of True Inspiration.

Land was too high for most of the members, who were in moderate circumstances. To purchase wood was costly, and there was no coal to be had. Rent for estates and factories was exorbitant, and increased every year. During the summer of 1841, no rain fell, so absolutely nothing was raised. The landlord wanted his rent as usual, regardless of the failure of crops. Everything seemed dark and dreary, for the leaders of the society were unable to meet the demands for money.

One day, as Christian Metz was walking over a hill, absorbed in meditation as to the future outlook of the society, he came within sight of the mills and estates that had been rented. He heard the hum of the machinery; he saw the toiling workmen bending under their heavy loads; he saw the little children playing and shouting around the house doors; he saw the women in the adjoining fields bending over the sheaves, sickles in hand, trying to get something, even the straw in return for the summer's work. While he stood there absorbed in thought, something "opened itself to him as if a ray of light suddenly burst from heaven." He felt that one hand was still powerful. "If they only could have faith in that divine Hand, all would be taken from the land of bondage to a land of freedom, equality and fraternity." Christian Metz told some of his friends about this sudden glimpse into the future. Others said they had had similar feelings, but dared not express them.

On the 21st of July, 1842, one of the members became inspired, and it seemed to him that the members should all leave their native land and should settle in one place, live under the same laws, and adopt a "community of goods" which then had many admirers in Europe. This movement had been caused by the appearance of E. Cabet's book on Communism, called *The Voyage and Adventures of Lord Caudal in Icaria*, a book much like More's *Utopia*. Still more prominent was Fourierism which had become universal.

All the elders were summoned to meet at Armenburg, where they discussed the matter thoroughly but came to no decision. Another meeting was held at Engelthal, where this important matter was again discussed. It was plain enough to them that they would have to leave Germany on account of the severe measures of the government and the failure of the crops of the preceding year, which had depleted their finances. They were still undecided where to go, but it seemed that the United States offered the best advantages.

On the 14th of August, 1842, the elders decided that four men should be elected to look up a place for them in America or any other country suitable for a new home, where they could all live in common.

The four men selected for this difficult and responsible task were Christian Metz, G.A. Weber, Wilhelm Noe and Gottlieb Ackermann, in whose hands was placed all power to act in matters concerning a suitable place and concerning the amount of land to be purchased.

After a love-feast held at Armenburg, they bade all others farewell

18

on the 5th of September, 1842. It was an affecting sight to see a thousand people or more assembled; in this large gathering everyone shed tears, feeling that all would soon follow these leaders into a foreign land, where they knew hardships without number must be endured.

The four, along with Weber's son Ferdinand, sailed September 20th on the *New York*. The ship reached New York October 26, 1842. On the advice of a land agent, they first traveled to and considered buying land in Chautauqua County, New York, near Erie, Pennsylvania. Travel in winter was difficult, and they decided not to buy the land because it was too far away from available markets. They next heard about an Indian reservation near Buffalo, New York, which was soon be be vacated by the Seneca tribe. They investigated the property purchased from the government by the Ogden Land Company, and entered into a contract with Joseph Fellows, an Ogden agent, for 10,000 acres at $10.50 an acre.

The contract was sent to Ogden to be signed, but he refused to recognize the sale Fellows had made. Metz, Ackermann, Weber and Noe, with Dorsheimer as interpreter, now had to go to Geneva to see Fellows; he could do nothing about the matter, but told them to see Wadsworth & Sons of Geneseo, who owned the controlling interest in the company. The Wadsworths were very courteous, but said that land had risen in value and that it would be impossible to sell at the figures Fellows had given them; still, if Ogden was willing to sell at that price, they would confirm the contract. They then returned to Buffalo to wait for a reply from Ogden.

By January 1843, they had received no answer, and they wrote to him that they would look for land farther west as they could wait no longer. Mr. Ogden immediately required them to come to New York City where all the stockholders were to be present at a meeting and might grant them favorable terms. Once more they left Buffalo, but with small hope of any agreement. On the journey they discussed the feasibility of the undertaking. Noe thought 4,000 acres would be enough, while Metz maintained that the amount they had bargained for was not too much. They finally made concessions on both sides and put the amount down to 5,000 acres, which amount, after much discussion and wrangling on the part of the Land Company, was bought for $10.50 per acre, setting the limit this time within six miles of Buffalo. It would have been better if they had bought the 10,000 acres, for nearly all this same land was afterwards purchased at a much higher price. They wrote to Germany rejoicing over their good fortune, but they were ignorant of the trials which were to be endured before the land could be called their own.

The Indians, as soon as they heard of the sale, began to show signs of hostility. Perhaps it is due to this fact that there had been so few buyers, for the people around Buffalo knew Indian character too well.

After this purchase, Metz and Ackermann made a visit to Galion, Crawford County, Ohio, where there existed a small society of Germans, many of whom they had known in the Fatherland.

On their return they found that fifty of their number had already arrived from Germany. No preparation had been made to receive them, for they were not expected until later. The men were set to work erecting houses, while the older people and the women were permitted to stay in the old log huts which the Indians had abandoned.

In 1843, the settlers laid out three villages. Members came in parties of fifty throughout the year. They built houses, schools, a sawmill and a large meetinghouse.

The Indians were enraged as they saw these people planting and building and threatened to make short work of them, and the settlers applied to Fellows, the land agent, who had promised that the Indians should soon depart for the West. Fellows arrested a few Indians because they hauled and sold wood which belonged to the Ebenezer community. The Indians in return claimed that the community had no deed to the land and therefore had no right to cut trees on it.

Matters went from bad to worse, and finally a council of arbitration was decided upon. Metz, Noe, and Weber appeared for the community, and John Seneca with his chiefs and Osborne, their lawyer, represented the Indians.

The Indians wanted to be paid for their land a second time, to which the community would not consent, for the land company had bought both the government right and the Indian claim. The Indians, incited by bad white men and poor whiskey, would not make concessions, and thus ended the first congress of peace without accomplishing any result.

By the end of 1843, three hundred and fifty persons had arrived.

Those remaining in Germany were trying to dispose of their property, but they were not successful. The landlords at Laubach and Budingen were unwilling to take back their estates when they heard that the members were about to leave. The members in America needed money to pay for the land, but none could be raised, since they were unable to sell their German property at any price.

In this crisis, C.L. Meyer from Zoar, Ohio, joined the community. He became of great value to them, as he knew English perfectly and also had a knowledge of law, which was of the utmost importance in the endless contest with the land company on one hand and the stubborn Indians on the other.

By April 1844, the purchase price for the reservation had to be at Washington. The Ogden Land Company could not meet the demand and thus fell back on the community, which by credit and loans, raised a sum of $50,000, which was sent to Washington. Still the community had no deed to the land. Becoming anxious about the title, Metz and Meyer went to New York City to investigate the matter. The land company could give no deed, since the title had not yet passed into their hands.

On their return to Buffalo they became still more discouraged at receiving a legal document from the attorneys of John Seneca, warning them to vacate the lands within one week or there would be trouble. To pay $50,000, nearly the entire sum, and then to be driven away seemed almost unendurable, but they did not know what to expect from the treacherous Indians.

Another council of arbitration was held, which resulted as unfortunately as the first, for the Indians were supported by able lawyers and had imbibed firewater so freely as to make the scene doubly interesting and exciting.

The community now appealed to the government at Washington. The Indians were ordered to leave for the homes assigned them in the West, but they were in no hurry and brought their case before the courts of New York. After a period of several years, the case was decided in favor of the Ebenezer community by Judge Hall.

This decision put an end to the Indian troubles, which had been very annoying; although they never led to bloodshed, feelings of intense hatred on the part of the Indians who were stirred up by many of the whites, placed the community in jeopardy if at any time an outbreak had occurred.

In June 1844, two-hundred-seventeen members came on the ship *Florida* via LeHavre, and in the following year, Wilhelm Morschell, Ernest Klein, G. Doller, C. Wilhelm, and many others came by the same route. This put an end to the emigration, and from this time on only a few came. More than eight hundred persons had come over, and all had found comfortable homes and were pleased both with the country and the communistic mode of life which the society had adopted.

Many remained in Germany, some because they were in good circumstances and were surrounded by relatives and friends with whom they could not part; in others, love of home and native land were too strong....The communication between the two countries ceased by degrees....due to the fact that the members in Germany fell away, and the younger ones did not follow in the steps of their fathers.

The majority of the members who had come to America belonged to the sturdy peasant class of Germany, that class which forms the "bone and marrow" of all governments. They came to this land of freedom to adopt an entirely new mode of life; they had no experience in this new scheme which they wanted to adopt; they had but scanty means; they knew nothing of the language, the laws or business methods of the country; still they possessed one advantage over the other societies which had adopted similar methods; the leaders of this society were neither agitators nor theorists—like Cabet and Owen—but they were sagacious, farsighted men, with much practical knowledge, something worth more than all the high-flown speculative theories in existence....

Notwithstanding their prosperity at Ebenezer, the elders preferred another locality where cheaper land could be obtained, and in 1855 the society elected C.M. Winzenried, John Beyer, Jacob Wittmer and Friedrich Heinemann to go west in search of a favorable place.

They chose Iowa. The number of members in Iowa recorded from January 1, 1861–January 1, 1891, is as follows: (1861) 572 members; (1871) 1,466 members; (1881) 1,521 members; (1890) 1,660 members; (1891) 1,688 members.

COMMUNAL SOCIETY

Iowa As It Is: Pen Sketches of Town and Country

The Towns on the C.R.I. & P.R.R.
The Amana Society
The Farms, Manufactures and Villages
The Canal and other Improvements
Religious Views of the Colony

Daily Gazette, Davenport, Iowa, June 29, 1867.
By the *Gazette* Special Correspondent

The Amana Society or Colony, as it is generally called, presents one of the most interesting examples in the United States of successful associated and cooperative labor. For this reason, no less than for its relation to the development of Iowa resources and wealth, a description of the Colony with an accurate presentation of facts obtained by personal visitations and inquiries by our special correspondent can not fail to be of interest to the readers of the Gazette.

The Colony is located in the valley of the Iowa River, in Iowa County. Its territory embraces nearly the whole of Amana township (thirty-six square miles) and a part of Iowa township next adjoining on the south. The total of this area comprises between 50,000 and 60,000 acres, and additions are being steadily made to this by purchase of adjacent lands. Reaching the Colony from the east, the traveler stops at Homestead, 21 miles west of Iowa City and 75 from Davenport.

23

This is the eastern most station of the Society, and is located in Iowa township. The next and only additional railroad town is South Amana, six miles west of Homestead. Almost directly north and two miles distant from South Amana is the village of West Amana. One mile east of the last named village is "Amana Under-the-Hill." Three and a half miles farther east is "Middle Amana." East of this, and two miles distant is Amana or "Main Amana." Still farther east one mile is "Little Amana."

This line of villages commencing with West Amana and ending with Little Amana, lies along under the bluffs which, running parallel to the Iowa River, forms the northern boundary of the Iowa Valley. The railroad is located on the south side of the stream. The Iowa river flows between the railroad villages of South Amana and Homestead and the north line of these villages.

Two substantial bridges cross the river. Both of these very superior structures were erected by the Colony. The one on the road from South Amana to West Amana cost $2,500. The county supervisors recently showed their appreciation of this structure, which is located on a county road, by voting $1,000 toward defraying the cost of erection. The other bridge is situated on the road running north from Homestead to Main Amana and was built entirely at the expense of the Colony at a cost of about $2,500. Thus the visitor who makes a tour of the Colony by going first to Homestead, then to South Amana, thence to West Amana, thence along the line of villages to Little Amana, thence again to Homestead, very nearly follows the lines of a parallelogram, the northern line of which nearly marks the center of the Colony tract, while the southern line is nearly that of the Colony's south boundary.

This tract is very largely composed of "bottom" land, lying along either bank of the Iowa. Most of this area is devoted to pasturage and meadow. The cultivated land is mostly on the higher and rolling prairies, on the bluffs which bound the valley of the Iowa. The soil is of the excellent black loam variety that characterizes the greater part of central Iowa. The crops raised are of wheat, barley, oats, corn, etc. No grain is raised for exportation except barley, which is successfully "pearled" by an ingenious process and thus marketed for the benefit of lovers of the best quality of "pearl barley." Flour is also largely exported from the mills, hereafter to be noticed. Nor are any cattle raised for foreign markets. Wool is extensively raised, but is manufactured before exportation.

Homestead is the shipping point for the entire colony. Here are received all supplies from abroad for the various villages, and here is the only post office. The railroad depot building built of brick was with the whole right of way for the road for the distance of six miles, until quite recently, the property of the Colony. There is here a steam sawmill, a fine lumberyard and nearby a brickyard, all primarily for the use of the Colony, but still selling brick and lumber to the settlers. There is also a country store, now having goods on hand to the amount of $30,000. It is a model establishment, and, in the variety and quality of goods, gives better satisfaction than country stores usually do.

A wholesale warehouse built of brick furnishes storage for all the marketable manufactures designed for shipment, and for all the supplies received from abroad for the Colony. A tin shop manufactures goods for the stores and settlement. There is also a shoe shop, blacksmith shop, wagon and harness shop, conducted on the same plan as the store and mill. The residences, and other buildings...are, with few exceptions, of brick and built in the most substantial manner, with especial reference to adaptation and comfort. As no attempt has here been made to build up a "town" in the American and popular acceptation of that term, Homestead presents an entirely different appearance from that of any other railroad village in the state. The buildings, as at the other villages in the Colony, are located mainly with a view to convenience. The population of Homestead is 160.

South Amana has neither post office nor railroad station—only a side track where the western-bound freight awaits the arrival of the eastern-bound express. Below the railroad is the Colony steam sawmill. On the hill south of the railroad are the barns and stables. These comprise nearly all the buildings that can be seen from the cars. The village proper is laid out on either side of the road (running south from the railroad and crossing the Iowa River to West Amana) and over the hill and out of sight of railroad travelers. On the eastern side of this road, and principal street of the village, are the blacksmith shop, wagon shop, cooper shop, etc. Here also are a large bake house, wash house and brew house, in which buildings the baking, washing and brewing of the entire village are regularly attended to.

On the western side of the road are two square blocks, the outer lines of which are filled by thirteen of the sixteen large brick dwellings in the village, two chapels—one on each square—and a country store, in which a large amount of business is transacted. A schoolhouse and teacher's residence are attached to and constitute a part of one of the chapels' edifice.

Each of these squares has in its center a large plat of ground which is common property to all residents on the square, and is made in some sort a joint stock kitchen garden. To each dwelling is allotted a large garden "patch," separated from its neighbors only by neat paths and rows of currant bushes. Thus the only fence on the square is that erected on its outer borders. The gardens thus enclosed are tended mainly by women. Nowhere else have we seen such cultivation. Nowhere such successful gardening. Here is every variety of vegetables, far in advance of the season, or at least in advance of the products of the neighboring counties at this time of year. Of the smaller fruits, there is also great abundance—currants, gooseberries, cherries, plums, etc., are or promise to be abundant. Grape vines train in luxuriant growth against the walls of the dwellings and over trellises. Several hundred hardy pear trees and apple trees in full bearing add their tribute to the wealth of the community which give evidence of the industry and thrift of the colonists.

There also we saw a large flock of sheep from which 2,400 pounds of wool were sheared last season.

In the sixteen dwelling houses there reside about one hundred and fifty persons. Twenty-two people are attending school. Some of these are in families; others are simply boarders.

At this village your correspondent went to a meeting, while staying overnight. What he saw and heard the reader will be informed when we speak of the religious peculiarities of the colony.

West Amana, two miles north of South Amana, has eighteen dwellings, located on squares and rejoicing in highly cultivated gardens and abundant shrubbery, and having the same general characteristics as South Amana. Here, however, the buildings are mostly of stone instead of brick. The number of inhabitants, shops etc. is about the same as at the southern village. An important feature in West

Amana, and one that gives to much superiority over the neighbors, is a flour mill, built of stone, and fitted up in a very superior manner. This fine mill has three runs of stone, and is worked by steam except in wet seasons and during high water, when a small creek is turned to good account in furnishing motive power. A windmill is also in successful operation moving machines for the manufacture of furniture and for other light work. A quarry close to the village furnishes excellent stone for building purposes....

Amana, Under-the-Hill or "against the hill," as some of the colonists phrase it, is snugly ensconced at the ridge or bluff which separates the bottom lands of Iowa from the upper. Indeed, all of the Amana villages are built on or close to one or the other of these ridges skirting either side of the Iowa valley.

There are fourteen dwellings of somewhat the same character... accommodating 130 residents. The store at this point is the least important in the Society, being located so far within the Colony as to be nearly cut off from outside trade. Here also are two chapels and a well-kept school with few pupils. (Here let it be noted, that children do not appear to be at all numerous in any part of the colony.) The buildings differ here from those of the other villages. Half of them are of stone and half of them frame. All of them are very large and roomy and are surrounded by the same well-kept and spacious yards, with the same wealth of shrubbery and dense foliage common to other villages.

Middle Amana is situated upon a level space of the ridge, which here projects far out into the bottom. At the foot of this ridge is the woolen mill, built of brick, three stories high, 110 feet long and 44 feet wide. This mill is a very superior structure and fitted up in the best possible manner. The particulars of its manufactures etc. will be embodied in the account of the woolen mill at Main Amana, both mills being practically united as one establishment.

Middle Amana is the second village of the colony in importance and population. The residences—some of brick, some stone, some frame—are built on squares and have exquisitely cultivated and adorned gardens, and orchards, and shrubberies, as have those at the other villages.

A distinguishing feature of this village is the colony printing and bindery office. Bills, receipts, checks, orders, etc. are printed and bound, as also are hymnbooks from stereotyped plates procured in Buffalo. No newspaper is printed or apparently desired.

Two miles east we reach Amana or Main Amana, the principal village of the colony. Here reside the President, Mr. Wizenried, and the secretary, Mr. John Byers, and about 400 inhabitants. The town is built partly on the ridge where the store is situated and partly on the bottom near to the factory and mill. This woolen mill is of the same size as the one at Middle Amana—110 feet by 44, three stories high, built of stone and having a wing in which the wool is sorted and washed, a separate building where the wool is received and a drying house, built of brick and 105 feet long. Together the two mills run six sets of cards, eight spinning jacks, twenty looms, mostly wide ones, and sixteen-hundred spindles, and work up each 170,000 pounds of wool. Work for these woolen mills comes from a long distance. In some instances parties have come 150 miles by wagon, to get carding done or to exchange their wool for the yarns and flannels made here. To accommodate these parties, a hotel and barn is necessary. These the Colony has provided, and during our visit it was well patronized.

Near to the woolen mill is a grist mill with four runs of stone, and a brick building fitted up with lathes for turning iron with forges and other appearances of a regular machine shop. The same power is used for both woolen and grist mills and the machine shop. They are usually run by steam being connected with a 50-horsepower engine of superior manufacture. There is however a small stream, "Brice Creek," which having been diverted from its natural course, is used in times of high water to run this machinery.

In a factory near the woolen mill, white cotton cloth, brought hither from the East, is dyed blue and printed with different patterns. This is run by a 20-horsepower engine which also runs the sorghum mill, and is used to saw wood, all the firewood of the settlement being cut by steam. The threshing, too, is performed by this same power. Several large barns are located near this mill, in which the oats are stored and are threshed during the winter; the straw being fed out to the cattle. The wheat is hauled to the machine (a Dubuque thresher), made in Davenport, direct from the field, a load being put through every ten minutes.

There is also at Amana a steam sawmill and a planing and matching mill, all in one building.

There is in Amana one large audience room, capable of containing all the people of the Colony, but this is not often used. There are also four chapels in Amana and these, as at other villages, are used every day. At the schoolhouse the number of children in attendance is about thirty. These are all under fourteen years of age.

A bakery, milk wagon and butcher shop in this, as in the other villages, perform their functions for all alike.

A "feature" at Main Amana, at least to your correspondent, is the morning milking of the 150 cows, which help contribute to the wealth of the Colony. When the milking is completed, the lacteal fluid is placed in tin cans, which are forthwith carried around to the houses in a one-horse wagon, the driver duly ringing his bell in truly metropolitan style. There is, however, no demand for "stamps" or "tickets." The boy driver understands his business, and gives to each house its "portion" in due season.

At South Amana our correspondent saw the product of fifty cows all disposed of in this way, before six o'clock in the morning.

The last and least of these villages is distant one mile from Amana and has about one-hundred inhabitants, but no store or mill. It has, however, a large brick chapel—well-used. The population is almost wholly engaged in agricultural pursuits. Here are kept or cared for most of the sheep belonging to the colony.

The Manufactures

The manufactures of these seven villages deserve particular notice. The flannels and yarns of the Amana Society are held in high esteem by the trade generally. Hence orders are continually filled here for Cincinnati, Buffalo, New York, Philadelphia and Boston, besides those from Davenport and from all the "region round about." The brand of the Society on any article is known to be a sure guarantee of texture, make, weight, etc. being just as represented.

Buckets, churns, tubs etc. are made in large quantities and sold to the farmers of the surrounding country.

Agriculture

The farm management of the colony might, in many particulars, be cited as an example to all agriculturists who would be successful. The soil is thoroughly cultivated. Weeds are kept remarkably scarce, the women work in the fields and make vigorous use of the hoe and rake. The best of agricultural machinery is used whenever practical—reapers, threshers, shelters etc. are here to be found of the best make. Large and substantial barns carefully shelter all the products of the field. Nothing is allowed to run to waste, rot, or to be lost or injured.

The Canal

A noteworthy and really gigantic work of internal improvement is now in progress, in the construction of a canal from the Iowa River, at a point about one mile west of West Amana. This canal is to run east along the entire length of the villages on the north of the railroad, a distance of seven miles, emptying into "Price Creek," and then carrying its waters into the Iowa again. When completed this canal will secure a fall of fourteen feet and an abundant flow of water all through the year, thus creating one of the best water powers in the state. The cost of this undertaking will be at least $50,000. A steam dredge, costing $10,000, is now steadily digging away eastward from the Iowa.

Religious History and Peculiarities

This colony is composed of a religious sect who style themselves "Direct Inspirationists." They claim to be under the direct inspiration of the Holy Spirit and acknowledged ecclesiastical head or leader—no bishop, no pastor, no elder. The sect originated in Germany about the year 1714, but the cooperation or community plan was not adopted until their establishment in the United States about the year 1842 when they located near Buffalo, New York. Disliking so near proximity to so large a city and being unable there to procure sufficient land, it was determined in 1843, to seek a location in the West. The work of removal occupied ten years and now, as has been seen, the 6,000 acres near Buffalo has been exchanged for nearly 60,000 in one of the most fertile counties of Iowa.

Belief and Practice

This sect is an offshoot of the Lutheran Church. They believe in the scriptures in the most literal interpretation. They hold to the necessity of repentance and faith and accept Christ as Savior and Mediator. The ordinance of baptism is not administered at all, the baptism of the Holy Ghost alone being deemed efficacious. The Lord's Supper is administered very seldom; perhaps years at a time will elapse before the community feels in a proper state of mind, or heart, to partake. The most solemn heart searching and preparation being deemed necessary.

Upon these occasions they also wash each other's feet. In their religious opinions they are very tolerant, having suffered in Germany a great deal of persecution for which cause mainly they fled to this country, they seem quite willing to live without any attempt to regulate the opinions of others or to make proselytes to their own views....

These colonists are evidently industrious, virtuous and devout. They sacredly respect and cherish the married relations. The nature of the life led does not, however, conduce to a multiplicity of marriages and seems almost wholly to prevent that intimacy between the sexes that is usually an indispensable precursor to nuptial union. A large number of both sexes are unmarried, and in their simple manner of life and rigid observance of religious duties, have fewer temptations to abandon a state of celibacy.

Of the sincerity, earnestness and piety of these people...Their devout faith, the cardinal tenet of which is that "no man liveth unto himself, but all are brethren in Christ Jesus," undoubtedly furnishes the explanation of the wonderful success of their association. Their religion is evidently the bond of union.

We found upon inquiry that the elder persons were not only contented, but enthusiastic under the system which here prevails. The younger ones among the men sometimes get dissatisfied and branch out in the world for themselves, but invariably get back again to the sheltering influences they unwittingly left.

Although an industrious community, it cannot be said that they work hard. The skilled labor of the colony is monopolized by its members and about 140 men are hired for the various departments of the more drudging manual labor. These employees, by the way, much prefer work at the colony to the ordinary run of employers. The weaving, in other mills usually performed by women, is here given over to the men, the women preferring outdoor labor.

The Colony now numbers about 1,300 persons, all Germans. The affairs of the Community are managed by thirteen elders chosen annually on the afternoon of the general election. These choose a President and Secretary of their own number, and to this body of men, thus constituted, and representing all of the colonies, are intrusted all the business affairs of the Society.

Excerpts from

"The Amana Community"

The Communistic Societies of the United States: From Personal Visit and Observation

By Charles Nordhoff. Harper & Brothers Publishers, 1875.

(A former editor of *Harper's* and the *New York Evening Post*, Charles Nordhoff visited all the existing Utopian and communistic societies in the United States. *The Communistic Societies of the United States* is one of the most comprehensive references on the success or failure of those groups.)

I.

The "True Inspiration Congregations" *(Wahre Inspiration's Gemeinden)*, as they call themselves, form a communistic society in Iowa, seventy-four miles west of Davenport.

The society has at this time 1450 members, owns about 25,000 acres of land, lives on this land in seven different small towns, carries on agriculture and manufactures of several kinds, and is highly prosperous.

Its members are all German.

The base of its organization is religion; they are Pietists, and their religious head, at present a woman, is supposed by them to speak by direct inspiration of God....they call themselves "Inspirationists." ...

II. Historical

The "Work of Inspiration" is said to have begun far back in the eighteenth century. I have a volume, printed in 1785, which is called the *Thirty-sixth Collection of the Inspirational Records*, and gives an account of Brother John Frederick Rock's journeys and visits in the year 1719, wherein are recorded numerous utterances of the Spirit by his word of mouth to the faithful in Constance, Schaffhausen, Zurich, and other places.

They admit, I believe, that the "Inspiration" died out from time to time, but was revived as the congregation became more godly. In 1749, in 1772, and in 1776 there were especial demonstrations. Finally, in the year 1816, Michael Krausert, a tailor of Strasburg, became what they call an "instrument" (werkzeug), and to him were added several others: Philip Morschel, a stocking-weaver and a German; Christian Metz, a carpenter, and finally, in 1818, Barbara Heynemann (Heinemann), a "poor and illiterate servant-maid," an Alsatian *(eine arme ganz ungelehrte Dienstmagd).*

Metz, who was for many years, and until his death in 1867, the spiritual head of the society, wrote an account of the society from the time he became an "instrument" until the removal to Iowa. From this, and from a volume of Barbara Heinemann's inspired utterances, I gather that the congregation did not hesitate to criticize, and very sharply, the conduct of their spiritual leaders, and to depose them, and even expel them for cause. Moreover, they recount in their books, without disguise, all their misunderstandings. Thus it is recorded of Barbara Heinemann that in 1820 she was condemned to expulsion from the society, and her earnest entreaties only sufficed to obtain consent that she should serve as a maid in the family of one of the congregation, but even then it was forbidden her to come to the meetings. Her exclusion seems, however, to have lasted but a few months. Metz, in his "Historical Description," relates that this trouble fell upon Barbara because she had too friendly an eye upon the young men; and there are several notices of her desire to marry, as, for instance, under date of August, 1822, where it is related that "the Enemy" tempted her again with a desire to marry George Landmann. But "the Lord showed through Brother Rath, and also to her own conscience, that this step was against His holy will, and accordingly they did not marry, but did repent concerning it, and the Lord's grace was once more given her." But, like Jacob, she seems to have wrestled with the Lord, for later she did marry George Landmann, and, though they were for a while under censure, she regained her old standing as an "inspired instrument," came over to the United States with her husband, was for many years the assistant of Metz, and since his death has been the inspired oracle of Amana.

In the year 1822 the congregations appear to have attracted the attention of the English Quakers, for I find a notice that in December of that year they were visited by William Allen, a Quaker minister from London, who seems to have been a man of wealth. He inquired concerning their religious faith, and told them that he and his brethren at home were also subject to inspiration. He persuaded them to hold a meeting, at which, by his desire, they read the 14th chapter of John, and he told them that it was probable he would be moved by the Lord to speak to them. But when they had read the chapter, and while they waited for the Quaker's inspiration, Barbara Heinemann was moved to speak. At this, Allen became impatient and left the meeting, and in the evening he told the brethren that the Quaker inspiration was as real as their own, but that they did not write down what was spoken by their preachers; whereto he received for reply that it was not necessary, for it was evident that the Quakers had not the real inspiration, nor the proper and consecrated "instruments" to declare the will of the Lord; and so the Quaker went away on his journey home, apparently not much edified....

Grace before "meat" at Amana

...In 1854 they were "commanded by inspiration" to remove to the West. They selected Iowa as their new home, because land was cheap there, and in 1855, having made a purchase, they sent out a detachment to prepare the way.

It is a remarkable evidence of the prudence and ability with which they conduct their business affairs that they were able to sell out the

School House, Amana

whole of their eight-thousand-acre tract near Buffalo, with all their improvements, without loss. Usually such a sale is extremely difficult, because the buildings of a communistic society have peculiarities which detract from their value for individual uses. The Rappists, who sold out twice, were forced to submit to heavy loss each time. I do not doubt that several of the northern Shaker societies would have removed before this to better soil and climate but for the difficulty of selling their possessions at a fair price.

The removal from Eben-Ezer to Amana, however, required ten years. As they found purchases in one place they sent families to the other; meantime they do not appear to have found it difficult to maintain their organization in both.

III. Amana - 1874

"The name we took out of the Bible," said one of the officers of the society to me. They put the accent on the first syllable. The name occurs in the Song of Solomon, the fourth chapter and eighth verse: "Come with me from Lebanon, my spouse, with me from Lebanon: look from the top of Amana, from the top of Shenir and Hermon, from the lions' dens, from the mountains of the leopards."

Amana in Iowa, however, is not a mountain, but an extensive plain, upon which they have built seven villages, conveniently placed so as to command the cultivated land, and to form an irregular circle within their possessions. In these villages all the people live, and they are thus divided:

Name	Population	Business
Amana	450	Woolen-mill, saw and grist mill, and farming
East Amana	125	Farming
Middle Amana	350	Woolen-mill and farming
Amana near the Hill	125	Farming, saw-mill, and tannery
West Amana	150	Grist-mill and farming
South Amana	150	Saw-mill and farming
Homestead	135	Railroad station, a saw-mill, farming and general depot

The villages lie about a mile and a half apart, and each has a store at which the neighboring farmers trade, and a tavern or inn for the accommodation of the general public. Each village has also its shoe-makers', carpenters', tailors', and other shops, for they aim to produce and make, as far as possible, all that they use. In Middle Amana there is a printing-office, where their books are made.

The villages consist usually of one straggling street, outside of which lie the barns, and the mills, factories, and workshops. The houses are well built, of brick, stone, or wood, very plain, each with a sufficient garden, but mostly standing immediately on the street. They use no paint, believing that the wood lasts as well without. There is usually a narrow sidewalk of boards and brick, and the schoolhouse and church are notable buildings only because of their greater size. Like the Quakers, they abhor "steeple-houses," and their church architecture is of the plainest. The barns and other farm buildings are roomy and convenient. On the boundaries of a village are usually a few houses inhabited by hired laborers.

Each family has a house for itself; though when a young couple marry, they commonly go to live with the parents of one or the other for some years.

As you walk through a village, you notice that at irregular intervals are houses somewhat larger than the rest. These are either cook-houses or prayer-houses. The people eat in common, but for convenience's sake they are divided so that a certain number eat together. For Amana, which has four hundred and fifty people, there are fifteen such cooking and eating houses. In these the young women are employed to work under the supervision of matrons, and hither when the bell rings come those who are appointed to eat at each—the sexes sitting at separate tables, and the children also by themselves.

"Why do you separate men from women at the table?" I asked. "To prevent silly conversation and trifling conduct," was the answer.

Food is distributed to the houses according to the number of persons eating in each. Meal and milk are brought to the doors; and each cooking-house is required to make its own butter and cheese. For those whom illness or the care of small children keeps at home, the food is placed in neat baskets, and it was a curious sight to see, when the dinner bell rang, a number of women walking rapidly about the streets with these baskets, each nicely packed with food.

When the bell ceases ringing and all are assembled, they stand up in their places in silence for half a minute, then one says grace, and when he ends, all say, "God bless and keep us safely," and then sit down. There is but little conversation at table; the meal is eaten rapidly, but with decorum; and at its close, all stand up again, someone gives thanks, and thereupon they file out with quiet order and precision.

They live well, after the hearty German fashion, and bake excellent bread. The table is clean, but it has no cloth. The dishes are coarse but neat; and the houses, while well-built and possessing all that is absolutely essential to comfort according to the German peasants' idea, have not always carpets, and have often a bed in what New Englanders would call the parlor, and in general are for use and not ornament.

They breakfast between six and half-past six, according to the season, have supper between six and seven, and dinner at half-past eleven. They have besides an afternoon lunch of bread and butter and coffee, and in summer a forenoon lunch of bread, to which they add beer or wine, both homemade.

They do not forbid tobacco.

Each business has its foreman; and these leaders in each village meet together every evening, to concert and arrange the labors of the following day. Thus if any department needs for an emergency an extra force, it is known, and the proper persons are warned. The trustees select the temporal foremen, and give to each from time to time his proper charge, appointing him also his helpers. Thus a member showed me his "ticket," by which he was appointed to the care of the cows, with the names of those who were to assist him. In the summer, and when the work requires it, a large force is turned into the fields, and the women labor with the men in the harvest. The workmen in the factories are, of course, not often changed.

The children are kept at school between the ages of six and thirteen; the sexes do not sit in separate rooms. The school opens at seven o'clock, and the children study and recite until half-past nine. From that hour until eleven, when they are dismissed for dinner, they knit gloves, wristlets, or stockings. At one o'clock school reopens, and they once more attend to lessons until three, from which hour till half-past four they knit again. The teachers are men, but they are relieved by women when the labor-school begins. Boys as well as girls are required to knit. One of the teachers said to me that this work kept them quiet, gave them habits of industry, and kept them off the streets and from rude plays.

They instruct the children in musical notation, but do not allow musical instruments. They give only the most elementary instruction, the "three Rs," but give also constant drill in the Bible and in the Catechism. "Why should we let our youth study? We need no lawyers or preachers; we have already three doctors. What they need is to live holy lives, to learn God's commandments out of the Bible, to learn submission to his will, and to love him."

The dress of the people is plain. The men wear in winter a vest which buttons close up to the throat, coat and trousers being of the common cut.

The women and young girls wear dingy colored stuffs, mostly of the society's own make, cut in the plainest style, and often short gowns, in the German peasant way. All, even to the very small girls, wear their hair in a kind of black cowl or cap, which covers only the back of the head, and is tied under the chin by a black ribbon. Also all, young as well as old, wear a small dark-colored shawl or handkerchief over the shoulders and pinned very plainly across the breast.

This peculiar uniform adroitly conceals the marks of sex, and gives a singularly monotonous appearance to women.

The sex, I believe, is not highly esteemed by these people, who think it is dangerous to the Christian's peace of mind. One of their most esteemed writers advises men to "fly from intercourse with women, as a very highly dangerous magnet and magical fire." Their women work hard and dress soberly; all ornaments are forbidden. To wear the hair loose is prohibited. Great care is used to keep the sexes apart. In their evening and other meetings, women not only sit apart from men, but they leave the room before the men break ranks. Boys are allowed to play only with boys, and girls with girls. There are no places or occasions for evening amusements where the sexes might meet. On Sunday afternoons, the boys are permitted to walk in the fields, and so are the girls, but these must go in another direction. "Perhaps they meet in the course of the walk," said a member to me, "but it is not allowed." At meals and in their labors they are also separated. With all this care to hide the charms of young women, to make them, as far as dress can do so, look old and ugly, and to keep the young men away from them, love, courtship, and marriage go on at Amana as elsewhere in the world. The young man "falls in love," and finds ways to make his passion known to its object; he no doubt enjoys all the delights of courtship, intensified by the difficulties which his prudent brethren put in his way, and he marries the object of his affection, in spite of her black hood and her sad-colored little shawl, whenever he has reached the age of twenty-four.

For before that age he may not marry, even if his parents consent. This is a merely prudential rule. "They have few cares in life, and would marry too early for their own good—food and lodging being secured them—if there were not a rule upon the subject," said one of their wise men. No matter how early two young people agree to marry, the wedding is deferred until the man reaches the proper age.

And when at last the wedding day comes, it is treated with a degree of solemnity which is calculated to make it a day of terror rather than unmitigated delight. The parents of the bride and groom meet, with two or three of the elders, at the house of the bride's father. Here, after singing and prayer, that chapter of Paul's writings is read wherein, with great plainness of speech, he describes to the Ephesians and the Christian world in general the duties of husband and wife. On this chapter the elders comment "with great thoroughness" to the young people, and "for a long time," as I was told, and after this lecture, and more singing and prayer, there is a modest supper, whereupon all retire quietly to their homes.

The strictly pious hold that marriage should be made only by consent of God, signified through the "inspired instrument."

While the married state has thus the countenance and sanction of the society and its elders, matrimony is not regarded as a meritorious act. It has in it, they say, a certain large degree of worldliness; it is not calculated to make them more, but rather less spiritually minded—so think they at Amana—and accordingly the religious standing of the young couple suffers and is lowered. In the Amana church there are three "classes," orders or grades, the highest consisting of those who have manifested in their lives the greatest spirituality and piety. If the new-married couple should have belonged for years to this highest class, their wedding would put them down into the lowest, or the "children's order," for a year or two, until they had won their way back by deepening piety.

The civil or temporal government of the Amana communists consists of thirteen trustees, chosen annually by the male members of the society. The president of the society is chosen by the trustees.

This body manages the finances, and carries on the temporalities generally, but it acts only with the unanimous consent of its members. The trustees live in different villages, but exercise no special authority, as I understand, as individuals. The foremen and elders in each village carry on the work and keep the accounts. Each village keeps its own books and manages its own affairs, but all accounts are finally sent to the headquarters at Amana, where they are inspected, and the balance of profit or loss is discovered. It is supposed that the labor of each village produces a profit, but whether it does or not makes no difference in the supplies of the people, who receive every thing alike, as all property is held in common. All accounts are balanced once a year, and thus the productiveness of every industry is ascertained.

The elders are a numerous body, not necessarily old men, but presumably men of deep piety and spirituality. They are named or appointed by inspiration, and preside at religious assemblies.

In every village four or five of the older and more experienced elders meet each morning to advise together on business. This council acts, as I understand, upon reports of those younger elders who are foremen and have charge of different affairs. These in turn meet for a few minutes every evening, and arrange for the next day's work.

Women are never members of these councils, nor do they hold, as far as I could discover, any temporal or spiritual authority, with the single exception of their present spiritual head, who is a woman of eighty years. Moreover, if a young man should marry out of the society, and his wife should desire to become a member, the husband is expelled for a year—at the end of which time both may make application to come in, if they wish.

They have contrived a very simple and ingenious plan for supplying their members with clothing and other articles aside from food. To each adult male an annual allowance is made of from forty to one hundred dollars, according as his position and labor necessitates more or less clothing. For each adult female the allowance is from twenty-five to thirty dollars, and from five to ten dollars for each child.

All that they need is kept in store in each village, and is sold to the members at cost and expenses. When anyone requires an article of clothing, he goes to the store and selects the cloth for which he is charged in a book he brings with him; he then goes to the tailor, who makes the garment and charges him on the book an established price. If he needs shoes, or a hat, or tobacco, or a watch, everything is in the same way charged. As I sat in one of the shops, I noticed women coming in to make purchases, often bringing children with them, and each had her little book in which due entry was made. "Whatever we do not use is so much saved against next year, or we may give it away if we like," one explained to me, and added that during the war, when the society contributed between eighteen and twenty thousand dollars to various benevolent purposes, much of this was given by individual members out of the savings on their year's account.

Almost every man has a watch, but they keep a strict rule on vanities of apparel, and do not allow the young girls to buy or wear earrings or breastpins.

The young and unmarried people, if they have no parents, are divided around among the families.

They have not many labor-saving contrivances; though, of course, the eating in common is both economical and labor-saving. There is in each village a general wash-house, where the clothing of the unmarried people is washed, but each family does its own washing.

They have no libraries, and most of their reading is in the Bible, and in their own "inspired" records, which, as I shall show further on, are quite voluminous. A few newspapers are taken, and each calling among them receives the journal which treats of its own specialty. In general, they aim to withdraw themselves as much as possible from the world, and take little interest in public affairs. During the war they voted, "but we do not now, for we do not like the turn politics have taken"—which seemed to me a curious reason for refusing to vote.

Their members came originally from many parts of Germany and Switzerland; they have also a few "Pennsylvania Dutch." They have much trouble with applicants who desire to join the society, and receive, the secretary told me, sometimes dozens of letters in a month from persons of whom they know nothing, and not a few of whom, it seems, write, not to ask permission to join, but to say that they are coming on at once. There have been cases where a man wrote to say that he had sold all his possessions, and was then on the way, with his family, to join the association. As they claim to be not an industrial, but a religious community, they receive new members with great care, and only after thorough investigation of motives and religious faith, and these random applications are very annoying to them. Most of their new members they receive from Germany, accepting them after proper correspondence and under the instructions of "inspiration." When they believe them worthy they do not inquire about their means, and a fund is annually set apart by the trustees to pay the passage of poor families whom they have determined to take in.

Usually a neophyte enters on probation for two years, signing an obligation to labor faithfully, to conduct himself according to the society's regulations, and to demand no wages. If at the close of his probation, he appears to be a proper person, he is admitted to full membership, and if he has property, he is then expected to put this into the common stock, signing also the constitution, which provides that on leaving he shall have his contribution returned, but without interest.

There are cases, however, where a newcomer is at once admitted to full membership. This is where "inspiration" directs breach of the general rule, on the ground that the applicant is already a fit person.

Most of their members came from the Lutheran Church, but they have also Catholics, and I believe several Jews.

They employ about two hundred hired hands, mostly in agricultural labors, and these are all Germans, many of whom have families. For these they supply houses, and give them sometimes the privilege of raising a few cattle on their land.

They are excellent farmers, and keep fine stock, which they care for with German thoroughness, stall-feeding in the winter.

The members do not work hard. One of the foremen told me that three hired hands would do as much as five or six of the members. Partly this comes no doubt from the interruption to steady labor caused by their frequent religious meetings, but I have found it generally true that the members of communistic societies take life easy.

The people are of varying degrees of intelligence, but most of them belong to the peasant class of Germany, and were originally farmers, weavers, or mechanics. They are quiet, a little stolid, and very well satisfied with their life. Here, as in other communistic societies, the brains seem to come easily to the top. The leading men with whom I conversed appeared to me to be thoroughly trained businessmen in the German fashion—men of education, too, and a good deal of intelligence. The present secretary told me that he had been, during all his early life, a merchant in Germany, and he had the grave and somewhat precise air of an honest German merchant of the old style—prudent, with a heavy sense of responsibility, a little rigid, and yet kindly.

At the little inn, I talked with a number of the rank and file, and noticed in them great satisfaction with their method of life. They were, on the surface, the commoner kind of German laborers; but they had evidently thought pretty thoroughly upon the subject of communal living, and knew how to display to me what appeared to them its advantages in their society: the absolute equality of all men—"as God made us," the security for their families, the abundance of food, and the independence of a master.

It seems to me that these advantages are dearer to the Germans than to almost any other nation, and hence they work more harmoniously in communistic experiments. I think I noticed at Amana, and elsewhere among the German communistic societies, a satisfaction in their lives, a pride in the equality which the communal system secures, and also in the conscious surrender of the individual will to the general good, which is not so clearly and satisfactorily felt among other nationalities. Moreover, the German peasant is fortunate in his tastes, which are frugal and well fitted for community living. He has not a great sense of or desire for beauty of surroundings; he likes substantial living, but cares nothing for elegance. His comforts are not, like the American's, of a costly kind.

I think, too, that his lower passions are more easily regulated or controlled, and certainly he is more easily contented to remain in one place. The innkeeper, a little to my surprise, when by chance I told him that I had spent a winter on the Sandwich Islands, asked me with the keenest delight and curiosity about the trees, the climate, and the life there, and wanted to know if I had seen the place where Captain Cook, "the great circumnavigator of the world," was slain. He returned to the subject again and again, and evidently looked upon me as a prodigiously interesting person, because I had been fortunate enough to see what to him was classic ground. An American would not have felt one-half of this man's interest, but he would probably have dreamed of making the same journey some day. My kindly host sat serenely in his place, and was not moved by a single wandering thought.

They forbid all amusements—all cards and games whatever, and all musical instruments—"one might have a flute, but nothing more." Also they regard photographs and pictures of all kinds as tending to idol-worship, and therefore not to be allowed.

They have made very substantial improvements upon their property; among other things, in order to secure a sufficient water-power, they dug a canal six miles long and from five to ten feet deep, leading a large body of water through Amana. On this canal they keep a steam-scow to dredge it out annually.

As a precaution against fire, in Amana there is a little tower upon a house in the middle of the village, where two men keep watch all night.

They buy much wool from the neighboring farmers, and have a high reputation for integrity and simple plain-dealing among their neighbors. A farmer told me that it was not easy to cheat them, and that they never dealt the second time with a man who had in any way wronged them, but that they paid a fair price for all they bought, and always paid cash.

In their woolen factories they make cloth enough for their own wants and to supply the demand of the country about them. Flannels and yarn, as well as woolen gloves and stockings, they export, sending some of these products as far as New York. The gloves and stockings are made not only by the children, but by the women during the winter months, when they are otherwise unemployed.

At present they own about 3,000 sheep, 1,500 head of cattle, 200 horses and 2,500 hogs.

The society has no debt, and has a considerable fund at interest.

They lose very few of their young people. Some who leave them return after a few years in the world. Plain and dull as the life is, it appears to satisfy the youth they train up; and no doubt it has its rewards in its regularity, peacefulness, security against want, and freedom from dependence on a master.

It struck me as odd that in cases of illness they use chiefly homeopathic treatment. The people live to a hale old age. They had among the members, in March, 1874, a woman aged ninety-seven, and a number of persons over eighty.

They are non-resistants, but during the late war paid for substitutes in the army. "But we did wrongly there," said one to me, "it is not right to take part in wars even in this way."

To sum up: the people of Amana appeared to me a remarkably quiet, industrious, and contented population; honest, of good repute among their neighbors, very kindly, and with religion so thoroughly and largely made a part of their lives that they may be called a religious people.

IV. Religion and Literature

"If one gives himself entirely, and in all his life, to the will of God, he will presently be possessed by the Spirit of God."

"The Bible is the Word of God; each prophet or sacred writer wrote only what he received from God."

"In the New Testament we read that the disciples were 'filled with the Holy Ghost.' But the same God lives now, and it is reasonable to believe that He inspires his followers now as then, and that He will lead his people, in these days as in those, by the words of his inspiration."

"He leads us in spiritual matters, and in those temporal concerns which affect our spiritual life, but we do not look to Him for inspired directions in all the minute affairs of our daily lives. Inspiration directed us to come to America, and to leave Eben-Ezer for Iowa. Inspiration sometimes directs us to admit a newcomer to full membership, and sometimes to expel an unworthy member. Inspiration discovers hidden sins in the congregation."

"We have no creed except the Bible."

"We ought to live retired and spiritual lives, to keep ourselves separate from the world, to cultivate humility, obedience to God's will, faithfulness, and love to Christ."

"Christ is our head."

Such are some of the expressions of their religious belief which the pious and well-instructed at Amana gave me. They have published two Catechisms—one for the instruction of children, the other for the use of older persons. From these it appears that they are Trinitarians, believe in "justification by faith," hold to the resurrection of the dead, the final judgment, but not to eternal punishment, believing rather that fire will purify the wicked in the course of time, longer or shorter according to their wickedness.

They do not practice baptism, either infant or adult, holding it to be a useless ceremony not commanded in the New Testament. They celebrate the Lord's Supper, not at regular periods, but only when by the words of "inspiration," God orders them to do so, and then with peculiar ceremonies, which I shall describe further on.

As to this word "Inspiration," I quote here from the Catechism their definition of it:

"Question: Is it therefore the Spirit or the witness of Jesus which speaks and bears witness through the truly inspired persons?

"Answer: Yes; the Holy Ghost is the Spirit of Jesus, which brings to light the hidden secrets of the heart, and gives witness to our spirits that is the Spirit of truth.

"Question: How were these 'instruments' or messengers called?

"Answer: Inspired or new prophets. They were living trumpets of

God, which shook the whole of Christendom, and awakened many out of their sleep of security.

"Question: What is the word of inspiration?

"Answer: It is the prophetic word of the New Testament, or the Spirit of prophecy in the new dispensation.

"Question: What properties and marks of divine origin has this inspiration?

"Answer: It is accompanied by a divine power, and reveals the secrets of the heart and conscience in a way which only the all-knowing and soul-penetrating Spirit of Jesus has power to do; it opens the ways of love and grace, of the holiness and justice of God, and these revelations and declarations are in their proper time accurately fulfilled.

"Question: Through whom is the Spirit thus poured out?

"Answer: They must conform themselves in humility and childlike obedience to all the motions and directions of God within them; without care for self or fear of men, they must walk in the fear of God, and with attentive watchfulness for the inner signs of his leading; and they must subject themselves in every way to the discipline of the Spirit."

Concerning the Constitution of the Inspiration Congregations or communities, the same Catechism asserts that it "is founded upon the divine revelation in the Old and New Testament, connected with the divine directions, instructions, and determinations, general and special, given through the words of the true inspiration."

"Question: Through or by whom are the divine ordinances carried out in the congregations?

"Answer: By the elders and leaders, who have been chosen and nominated to this purposes by God.

"Question: What are the duties?

"Answer: Every leader or elder of the congregation is in duty bound, by reason of his divine call, to advance, in the measure of the grace and power given him, the spiritual and temporal welfare of the congregation; but in important and difficult circumstances the Spirit of prophecy will give the right and correct decision.

"Question: Is the divine authority to bind and loose, intrusted, according to Matt. XVI, 19, to the apostle Peter, also given to the elders of the Inspiration Congregations?

"Answer: It belongs to all elders and teachers of the congregation of the faithful, who were called by the Lord Jesus through the power of his Holy Spirit, and who, by the authority of their divine call, and of the divine power within them, rule without abuse the congregations or flocks intrusted to them.

"Question: What are the duties of the members of the Inspiration Congregations?

"Answer: A pure and upright walk in fear of God, heartfelt love and devotion toward their brethren, and childlike obedience toward God and the elders."

These are the chief articles of faith of the Amana Community.

They regard the utterances, while in the trance state, of their spiritual head as given from God; and believe—as is asserted in the Catechism—that evils and wrongs in the congregation will be thus revealed by the influence, or, as they say, the inspiration or breath of God; that in important affairs they will thus receive the divine direction, and that it is their duty to obey the commands thus delivered to them.

There were "inspired instruments" before Christian Metz. Indeed, the present "instrument," Barbara Landmann, was accepted before him, but by reason of her marriage fell from grace for a while. It would seem that Metz also was married; for I was told at Amana, that at this death in 1867, at the age of sixty-seven, he left a daughter in the community.

The words of "inspiration" are usually delivered in the public meetings, and at funerals and other solemn occasions. They have always been carefully written down by persons specially appointed to that office, and this appears to have been done as long ago as 1719, when "Brother John Frederick Rock" made his journey through Constance, Schaffhausen, Zurich, etc., with "Brother J.J. Schultes as writer, who wrote down everything correctly, from day-to-day, and in weal-or-woe."

When the "instrument" "falls into inspiration," he is often severely shaken—Metz, they say, sometimes shook for an hour—and thereupon follow the utterances which are believed to proceed from God. The "instrument" sits or kneels, or walks about among the congrega-

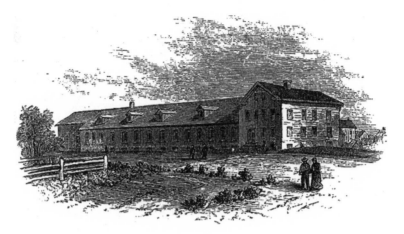

Church at Amana

tion. "Brother Metz used to walk about in the meeting with his eyes closed, but he always knew to whom he was speaking, or where to turn with words of reproof, admonition, or encouragement"—so I was told.

The "inspired" words are not always addressed to the general congregation, but often to individual members, and their feelings are not spared. Thus, in one case, Barbara Landmann, being "inspired," turned upon a sister with the words, "But you, wretched creature, follow the true counsel of obedience," and to another: "And you, contrary spirit, how much pain do you give to our hearts. You will fall into everlasting pain, torture, and unrest if you do not break your will and repent, so that you may be accepted and forgiven by those you have offended, and who have done so much for you."

The warnings, prophecies, reproofs, and admonitions thus delivered by the "inspired instrument," are all, as I have said, carefully written down, and in convenient time printed in yearly volumes, entitled "Year-Books of the True Inspiration Congregations: Witnesses of the Spirit of God, which happened and were spoken in the Meetings of the Society, through the Instruments, Brother Christian Metz and Sister B. Landmann," with the year in which they were delivered. In this country they early established a printing-press at Eben-Ezer, and after their removal, also in Iowa, and have issued a considerable number of volumes of these records. They are read as of equal authority and almost equal importance with the Bible. Every family possesses

Interior view of church

some volumes; and in their meetings extracts are read aloud after the reading of the Scriptures.

There is commonly a brief preface to each revelation, recounting the circumstances under which it was delivered, as for instance:

"No. 10. Lower Eben-Ezer, November 7, 1853.—Monday morning the examination of the congregation was made here according to the command of the Lord. For the opening service five verses were sung of the hymn, 'Lord, give thyself to me;' the remainder of the hymn was read. After the prayer, and a brief silence, Sister Barbara Landmann fell into inspiration, and was forced to bear witness in the following gracious and impressive revival words of love."

The phrase varies with the contents of the message, as, on another occasion, it is written that "both 'instruments' fell into inspiration, and were forced to bear witness in the following gracious and impressive revival words of love."

The phrase varies with the contents of the message, as on another occasion, it is written that "both 'instruments' fell into inspiration, and there followed this earnest admonition to repentance, and words of warning;" or, again, the words are described as "important," or "severe," or "gentle and gracious and hope inspiring...."

...The inspired utterances are for the most part admonitory to a holier life; warnings, often in the severest language, against selfishness, stubbornness, coldness of heart, pride, hatred toward God, grieving the Spirit with threats of the wrath of God, of punishment, etc.

Humility and obedience are continually inculcated. "Lukewarmness" appears to be one of the prevailing sins of the community. It is needless to say that to a stranger these homilies are dull reading. Concerning violations of the Ten Commandments or of the moral law, I have not found any mention here, and I do not doubt that the members of the society live, on the whole, uncommonly blameless lives. I asked, for instance, what punishment their rules provided for drunkenness, but was told that this vice is not found among them; though, as at Economy and in other German communities, they habitually use both wine and beer.

When any member offends the rules or order of life in the society, he is admonished *(ermahnt)* by the elders, and if he does not amend his ways, expulsion follows, and here as elsewhere in the communities I have visited, they seem vigilantly to purge the society of improper persons.

The following twenty-one "Rules for Daily Life," printed in one of their collections, and written by one of their older leaders, E.L. Gruber, give, I think, a tolerably accurate notion of their views of the conduct of life:

"I. To obey, without reasoning, God, and through God, our superiors.

"II. To study quiet, or serenity, within and without.

"III. Within, to rule and master your thoughts.

"IV. Without, to avoid all unnecessary words, and still to study silence and quiet.

"V. To abandon self, with all its desires, knowledge, and power.

"VI. Do not criticize others, either for good or evil, neither to judge nor to imitate them; therefore contain yourself, remain at home, in the house and in your heart.

"VII. Do not disturb your serenity or peace of mind—hence neither desire nor grieve.

"VIII. Live in love and pity toward your neighbor, and indulge neither anger nor impatience in your spirit.

"IX. Be honest, sincere, and avoid all deceit and even secretiveness.

"X. Count every word, thought, and work as done in the immediate presence of God, in sleeping and waking, eating, drinking, etc., and give Him at once an account of it, to see if all is done in his fear and love.

"XI. Be in all things sober, without levity or laughter, and without vain and idle words, works, or thoughts; much less heedless or idle.

"XII. Never think or speak of God without the deepest reverence, fear, and love, and therefore deal reverently with all spiritual things.

"XIII. Bear all inner and outward sufferings in silence, complaining only to God; and accept all from Him in deepest reverence and obedience.

"XIV. Notice carefully all that God permits to happen to you in your inner and outward life, in order that you may not fail to comprehend His will and to be led by it.

"XV. Have nothing to do with unholy, and particularly with needless business affairs.

"XVI. Have no intercourse with worldly-minded men; never seek their society; speak little with them, and never without need, and then not without fear and trembling.

"XVII. Therefore, what you have to do with such men, do in haste; do not waste time in public places and worldly society, that you be not tempted and led away.

"XVIII. Fly from the society of women-kind as much as possible, as a very highly dangerous magnet and magical fire.

"XIX. Avoid obeisance and the fear of men; these are dangerous ways.

"XX. Dinners, weddings, feasts, avoid entirely; at the best there is sin.

"XXI. Constantly practice abstinence and temperance, so that you may be as wakeful after eating as before."

These rules may, I suppose, be regarded as the ideal standard toward which a pious Inspirationist looks and works. Is it not remarkable that they should have originated and found their chief adherents among peasants and poor weavers?

Their usual religious meetings are held on Wednesday, Saturday, and Sunday mornings, and every evening. On Saturday, all the people of a village assemble together in the church or meetinghouse; on other days they meet in smaller rooms, and by classes or orders.

The society consists of three of these orders—the highest, the middle, and the lower, or children's order. In the latter fall naturally the youth of both sexes, but also those older and married persons whose religious life and experience are not deep enough to make them worthy of membership in the higher orders.

The evening meeting opens a little after seven o'clock. It is held in a large room specially maintained for this purpose. I accompanied one of the brethren, by permission, to these meetings during my stay at Amana. I found a large, low-ceiled room, dimly lighted by a single lamp placed on a small table at the head of the room, and comfortably warmed with stoves. Benches without backs were placed on each side of this chamber; the floor was bare, but clean, and hither entered, singly or by twos or threes, the members, male and female, each going to the proper place without noise. The men sat on one side, the women on the other. At the table sat an elderly man of intelligent face and a look of some authority. Near him were two or three others.

When all had entered and were seated, the old man at the table gave out a hymn, reading out one line at a time; and after two verses were sung in this way, he read the remaining ones. Then, after a moment of decorous and not unimpressive silent meditation, all at a signal rose and kneeled down at their places. Hereupon the presiding officer uttered a short prayer in verse, and after him each man in his turn, beginning with the elders, uttered a similar verse of prayer, usually four, and sometimes six lines long. When all the men and boys had thus prayed—and their little verses were very pleasant to listen to, the effect being of childlike simplicity—the presiding elder closed with a brief extemporary prayer, whereupon all arose.

Then he read some verses from one of their inspired books, admonishing to a good life; and also a brief homily from one of Christian Metz's inspired utterances. Thereupon all arose, and stood in their places in silence for a moment, and then, in perfect order and silence and with a kind of military precision, benchful after benchful of people walked softly out of the room. The women departed first, and each went home, I judge without delay or tarrying in the hall for when I got out the hall was already empty.

The next night the women prayed instead of the men, the presiding officer conducting the meeting as before. I noticed that the boys and younger men had their places on the front seats, and the whole meeting was conducted with the utmost reverence and decorum.

On Wednesday and Sunday mornings the different orders meet at the same hour, each in its proper assembly-room. These are larger than those devoted to the evening meetings. The Wednesday morning meeting began at half-past seven, and lasted until nine. There was, as in the evening meetings, a very plain deal table at the head, and benches, this time with backs, were arranged in order, the sexes sitting by themselves as before; each person coming in with a ponderous hymnbook, and a Bible in a case. The meeting opened with the singing of six verses of hymn, the leader reading the remaining verses. Many of their hymns have from ten to fourteen verses. Next he read some passages from one of the inspirational utterances of Metz; after which followed prayer, each man, as in the evening meetings, repeating a little supplicatory verse. The women did not join in this exercise.

Then the congregation got out their Bibles; the leader gave out the fifth chapter of Ephesians, and each man read a verse in his turn; then followed a psalm, and the women read those verses which remained after all the men had read. After this the leader read some further passages from Metz. After the reading of the New Testament chapter and the psalm, three of the leaders, who sat near the table at the head of the room, briefly spoke upon the necessity of living according to the words of God, doing good works and avoiding evil. Their exhortations were very simple and without any attempt at eloquence, in a conversational tone.

Finally another hymn was sung; the leader pronounced a blessing, and we all returned home, the men and women going about the duties of the day.

On Saturday morning, the general meeting is held in the church. The congregation being then more numerous, the brethren do not all pray, but only the elders; as in the other meetings, a chapter from the New Testament is read and commented upon by the elders; also passages are read from the inspired utterances of Metz or some other of their prophets, and at this time, too, the "instrument," if moved, falls into a trance, and delivers the will of the Holy Spirit.

They keep New Year's as a holiday, and Christmas, Easter, and the Holy-week are their greatest religious festivals. Christmas is a three days' celebration, when they make a feast in the church; there are no Christmas trees for the children, but they receive small gifts. Most of the feast days are kept double—that is to say, during two days. During the Passion week they have a general meeting in the church every day at noon, and on each day the chapter appropriate to it is read, and followed by prayer and appropriate hymns. The week ends, of course, on Sunday with the ascension, but on Easter Monday, which is also kept, the children receive colored eggs.

At least once in every year there is a general and minute *"Untersuchung,"* or inquisition of the whole community, including even the children—and examination of its spiritual condition. This is done by classes or orders, beginning with the elders themselves, and I judge, from the relations of this ceremony in their printed books, that it lasts long, and is intended to be very thorough. Each member is expected to make confession of his sins, faults, and shortcomings, and if any thing is hidden, they believe that it will be brought to light by the inspired person, who assumes on this occasion an important part, admonishing individuals very freely, and denouncing the sins and evils which exist in the congregation. At this time, too, any disputes which may have occurred are brought up and healed, and an effort is made to revive religious fervor in the hearts of all. Not unfrequently, the examination of a class is adjourned from day to day, because they are found to be cold and unimpressible; and I notice that on these occasions the young people in particular are a cause of much grief and trouble on account of their perverse hardness of heart.

The celebration of the Lord's Supper is their greatest religious event. It is held only when the "inspired instrument" directs it, which may not happen once in two years, and it is thought so solemn and important an occasion that a full account of it is sometimes printed in a book. I have one such volume: *"Das Liebes-und Gedachtniszmahl des Leidens und Sterbens unsers Herrn und Heilandes Jesu Christi, wie solches von dem Herrn durch Sein Wort und zeugnisz angekundigt, angeordnet und gehalten worden, in Vier Abtheilungen, zu Mittel und Nieder Eben-Ezer, im Jahr 1855."* ("The Supper of Love and Remembrance of the suffering and death of our Lord and Saviour Jesus Christ: How it was announced, ordered, and held by his word and witness, in four parts, in Middle and Lower Eben-Ezer, in the year

1855.") It is a neatly printed volume of 284 pages.

The account begins with the announcement of the Lord's command: "Middle Eben-Ezer, April 21st, 1855, Saturday, in the general meeting, in the beginning, when the congregation was assembled, came the following gracious words and determination of the Lord, through Brother Christian Metz." Thereupon, after some words of preface, the "instrument" kneeled down, the congregation also kneeling, and said: "I am commanded humbly to reveal, according to the sacred and loving conclusion, that you are to celebrate the supper of love and remembrance in the presence of your God. The beginning and the course of it shall be as before. There will be on this occasion humiliations and revelations, if in any the true Worker of righteousness and repentance has not been allowed to do his work. The Lord will make a representation of the lack of his understanding in many of you; his great love will come to light, and will light up everyone." After more of this kind of address, the "instrument" said: "You are to begin the Lord's Supper on Ascension-day, make ready then all your hearts, clean out all filth, all that is rotten and stinks, all sins and every thing idle and useless; and cherish pious thoughts, so that you shall put down the flesh, as you are commanded to," and so on.

On a following Sunday, the "instrument" recurred to the subject, and in the course of his remarks reproved one of the elders for disobedience to the Lord and resistance to grace, and displaced him in the assembly, calling another by name to his place. At the close, he spoke thus, evidently in the name and with the voice of God: "And I leave it to you, my servants, to take out the middle order here and there, some into the first and out of the third into the second, but not according to favor and prejudice, but according to their graces and conduct, of which you are to take notice."

A day was given to admonitions and preparation; the "instrument," speaking not only to the congregation in general in the morning and afternoon meetings, but to a great many in particular—admonishing, exhorting, blaming, encouraging them by name. The next morning there was a renewal of such hortatory remarks, with singing and prayer, and in the afternoon, all being prepared, the elders washed the feet of the brethren. This is done only in the higher orders.

Thereupon tables are brought in, and bread and wine are placed.

After singing, the "inspired" person blesses these, and they are then received by the brethren and sisters from the hands of the elders, who pronounce the customary words of Scripture.

This being accomplished, the assembly temporarily adjourns, and persons previously appointed for this office spread on the tables a modest supper of bread and cake, coffee, chocolate, and a few other articles of food, and to this all sit down with solemn joy. At the conclusion of this meal, a hymn is sung, and the assembly retires to their homes.

When the three regular orders have gone through this celebration, there is a fourth, consisting of children under sixteen years, and of certain adult members who for various reasons have been thought unworthy to partake with the rest, and these also go through a thorough examination.

I asked one of their leading elders whether they believed in a "prayer-cure," explaining what the Oneida communists understand by this phrase. He replied, "No, we do not use prayer in this way, to cure disease. But it is possible. But if God has determined death, ten doctors cannot help a man."

The present inspired instrument being very aged, I asked whether another was ready to take her place. They said no, no one had yet appeared, but they had no doubt God would call someone to the necessary office. They were willing to trust Him, and gave themselves no trouble about it.

It remains to speak of their literature.

They have a somewhat ponderous hymnology, in two great volumes, one called *The Voice from Zion: to the Praise of the Almighty,* by John William Petersen (A.D. 1698), printed at Eben-Ezer, New York, in 1851, and containing 958 pages. The hymns are called Psalms, and are not in rhyme. They are to be sung in a kind of chant, as I judge from the music prefixed to them; and are a kind of commentary on the Scripture, one part being taken up with the Book of Revelation.

The other volume is the hymnbook in regular use. It contains 1285 pages, of which 111 are music—airs to which the different hymns may be sung. The copy I have is of the third edition, and bears the imprint, "Amana, Iowa, 1871." Its title is *Psalms after the manner of David,* *for the children of Zion.* It has one peculiarity which might, with advantage, be introduced in other hymnbooks. Occasional verses are marked with an asterisk (*), and it is recommended to the reader that these be taught to the children as little prayers. In practice, I found that in their evening meetings the grown persons, as well as the children, recited these simple and devotional little verses as their prayers, surely a more satisfactory delivery to them and the congregation than rude and halting attempts at extemporary utterance.

Many of the hymns are very long, having from twelve to twenty-four verses; and it is usual at their meetings to sing three or four verses and then read the remainder. They do not sing well, and their tunes—those at least which I heard—are slow, and apparently in a style of music now disused in our churches. The hymns are printed as prose, only the verses being separated. I was told that they were "all given by the Spirit of God," and that Christian Metz had a great gift of hymn-writing, very often, at home or elsewhere, writing down an entire hymn at one sitting. They are all deeply devotional in spirit, and have not unfrequently the merit of great simplicity and a pleasing quaintness of expression, of which I think the German language is more capable than our ruder and more stubborn English.

Their writers are greatly given to rhyming. Even in the inspirational utterances, I find frequently short admonitory paragraphs where rude rhymes are introduced. Among their books is one, very singular, called "Innocent Amusement" *("Unschuldiges Zeitvertreib"),*...It is a collection of verses, making pious applications of many odd subjects. Among the headings I found: "Cooking," "Rain," "Milk," "The Ocean," "Temperance," "Salve," "Dinner," "A Mast," "Fog," "A Net," "Pitch," "A Rainbow," "A Kitchen," etc., etc. It is a mass of pious doggerel, founded on Scripture and with fanciful additions.

Another is called *Jesus's ABC, for His Scholars,* and is also in rhyme. Another is entitled *Rhymes on the Sufferings, Death, Burial, and Resurrection of Christ.* There are about twelve hundred pages of the ABC book. They have printed also a miniature Thomas à Kempis, *For the Edification of Children;* two catechisms; a little work entitled *Treasure for Those Who Desire God,* and other works of similar character....

At the end of the Catechism are some pages of rules for the conduct of children at home, in church, at school, during play hours, at meals, and in all the relations of their lives. Many of these rules are excellent, and the whole of them might well be added to the children's catechisms in use in the churches. Piety, orderly habits, obedience, politeness, cleanliness, kindness to others, truthfulness, cheerfulness, etc., are all inculcated in considerable detail, with great plainness of speech, and in sixty-six short paragraphs, easily comprehended by the youngest children. The fifty-fourth rule shows the care with which they guard the intercourse of the sexes: "Have no pleasure in violent games or plays; do not wait on the road to look at quarrels or fights; do not keep company with bad children, for there you will learn only wickedness. Also, do not play with children of the other sex."

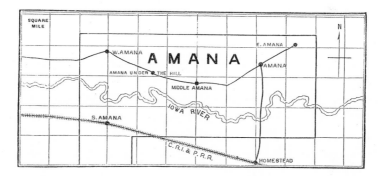

AMANA vor der Höhe.

von der Südseite.

The History of Iowa County

Union Historical Company, Birdsall, Williams & Co., Des Moines, Iowa, 1881. From: Iowa County Historical Society Reprint, 1982.

Amana Township

The word "Amana" means "believe true" or "remain true." This is a noble motto, and the history of the colony shows that the sentiment contained in that name has not been unworthily bestowed. The Holy Bible is the foundation of their faith and practice.

Statistics

The population of this township, according the United States census for 1880, was 1,633, being an increase during the last decade of 192. There are in the township 233 polls, but at the presidential election, November 2, 1880, only forty-three votes were cast. For James A. Garfield, 22 votes; W.S. Hancock, 19 votes, and J.B. Weaver, 2 votes, showing unmistakably that these quiet, unassuming German colonists do not desire to take an active part in our national politics. They raise domestic animals in large numbers both for farm use and the market. There are cattle to the number of 1,256, horses 206, sheep 3,190, and swine 1,088. The taxable value of merchandise in their several villages, excluding Homestead, is $35,000, and the capital employed in manufacturing in the said six villages is over $85,000. The personal property of all kinds is over $189,000, and if we estimate the personalty of Homestead at $25,000, which is certainly low enough, we have the personal property of the corporate colony at $214,000, which is over $50,000 more than last year's assessed valuation of personalty of Marengo city and Marengo township combined. The realty of Amana township is assessed at $215,000.

Schools

There are in this township two ungraded schools and five graded schools. There are two departments in each of the graded schools. There are twelve male teachers who teach twelve months in the year, schools being in session all the year round. They are paid an average salary of $20 per month. The children and youth between the ages of five and twenty-one are: males, 224; females, 222. The total enrollment in the schools, 427; with an average daily attendance of 343.

This shows the highest percentage of enrollment and average daily attendance of any township in the county. The average cost of tuition per month for each pupil is $1.25. The estimated value of school-houses in the township is $7,100, being more than that of any other except Marengo township.

They are unusually moral and law abiding. They are never known to quarrel and fight. Sober, industrious, moral, religious and happy— what a lesson of good citizenship we are taught by these Germans, who have adopted America for their home and that of their children. None of the family and common domestic relations of Christian people are surrendered to the corporation. Children are brought up at home and schooled at the public expense under competent teachers. A degree of honesty, intelligence, and enterprise is manifested there that puts to shame the smartness and trickery of many of our modern American towns.

An Iowa Commune

History and Habits of the Amana Society in Iowa

Cedar Rapids Gazette, October 1, 1883
By Des Moines Correspondent for the *New York Tribune*

The Amana society is the outgrowth of a small band of people who came to this country from the north of Germany in 1846. Their religion was one of peace. Their government demanded of every male person military service. This they refused to give. They were then imprisoned and their property sequestered. About forty of them came to this country and settled near Buffalo, New York, but soon afterward removed to this spot and named it Amana, which signifies "here we will rest." They purchased from the government a whole township, six miles square, through which runs the Iowa River, one of the largest streams in the state. They perfected an organization of the community and gave it the name of Amana Society, which is now incorporated under the laws of the state. All that each individual possessed was consolidated into common property. By the terms of the compact, there is no individual ownership of anything, with the slight exception for personal use.

The community is governed by a president and executive committee, elected by vote of the community. This committee has general supervision of all business of the society, elects the superintendents of the various departments of labor, and directs all its affairs. The president is simply an advisory officer and is selected for his age and mature judgment. He presides at meetings of the executive committee.

The Iowa River makes a large bend near the eastern boundary of the township. From the eastern deflection, a canal about ten feet wide was cut, five miles in length, through the village to the western point of deflection. Along this canal are located the residence lots, each lot abutting on the canal. The canal furnishes water for domestic use and watering the gardens. Each family has a house for its own use, surrounding the yards and a garden. Grapes are extensively grown, and palatable wine made from them, each family making its own supply.

Large boardinghouses are provided in each village (for there are now six villages) for the accommodation of the unmarried people. At those boardinghouses also the entire people take their meals. No cooking nor general housekeeping is done at the residences. There are appointed...persons to perform the various duties of the society: to oversee the boardinghouses and do the work therein, cooking, baking, laundry, scrubbing, carrying water, etc.; some care for the poultry, swine, sheep, horses, cattle; various kinds of farm work are set off to different persons—so in the mills, factories and shops.

Just before meal hours, a man will come to a boardinghouse with live poultry, which is at once taken and dressed; another will bring vegetables, another meat. After each meal, the garbage man comes around and all refuse is carried away, fed to swine or put in the compost heap. Each and every person has his or her allotted work, and all moves on in perfect system. There are no drones. There are large cotton and woolen mills, a starch factory and fruit-canning shops. The cotton goods made are the best and most durable to be found in the United States, and they get higher prices than eastern manufacturers. They sell all they can make to retail dealers in this and adjoining states, who have regular customers for them. So of their woolen goods, the stamp of the Amana society establishes their quality.

They are a thoroughly honest people. Whatever they do is well done. They are slow and plodding. They never get in a hurry. They retain many of the habits and customs of the fatherland. The older people still retain the quaint dress of their ancestors. The younger portion have Americanized themselves.

They are very devout people. Their religion is similar to that of the Quakers. They do not accept the New Testament. Marriage is a divine institution with them....The marriage ceremony is conducted always at the church, and is precisely like that of the Quakers.

Numerous applications are made to unite with them every year, but for several years all have been rejected, as they have as large a membership as they desire, the population being about 2,000. The society is immensely wealthy, and has no need of money.

At each village are immense barns and sheds where all hay and grain are stored,...Oxen are extensively used in farm work, being admirably suited to the plodding, easy-going ways of the people. The people are eminently social among themselves. They are courteous to strangers, but do not desire their presence, except for pure business.

A Story from History

Jesse James and Gang Robbed South Amana

Marengo Pioneer Republican, 1940 (about an 1877 event)

In 1940 Herman Shoup, farm manager at South Amana who was his party's nominee for county supervisor in the general election in November, brought a newspaper clipping to the Pioneer-Republican telling of when Jesse James and the Green Brothers robbed the South Amana store.

The clipping was dated Nov. 12, 1927, but recalled the robbery of April 27, 1877. The story was retold in 1927 at the time of the death of Emil Wolf, who worked in the store when the holdup took place.

Let's follow the action as told in the clipping. The tale:

In 1877 the general store at South Amana did a big business, drawing on a wide circle of a rather well-to-do farming population. This was before the Milwaukee railroad was built through there and before the Upper store and hotel had been established.

These flourishing business conditions seem to have been brought to the attention of Jesse James and his gang by accomplices known as the Green brothers, who lived on a farm near Marengo. Their adventurous bandit spirit was thereby aroused and they set to work to acquire a share of the profits made by these simple and industrious Amana folk.

The night of the robbery, April 27, 1877, was suitable for such a deed. It was dark and stormy with intermittent thunder showers. Emil Wolf and Charles Ratzel, who by the way, was later general business manager at South Amana, constituted the main help of the store.

These two 17-year-old lads had their room upstairs in the store building and their only protection was an empty .22 short revolver and a dog.

The gang of outlaws, as was confessed afterward by the Green brothers, came to South Amana that night in an open vehicle driven by one of the two brothers. They attacked the rear door of the north side of the store building and, finding it secured by a formidable homemade lock, disregarded a "jimmy"—and simply sawed the lock out.

In the meantime the dog inside kept up an incessant barking, which eventually aroused the two boys, Wolf and Ratzel, from their deep slumber.

Ratzel, after an argument with Wolf, stepped to a ventilator which communicated with the store room. He heard other suspicious noises besides the barking of the dog. (The dog by now had retired to the top of a high counter.)

Gathering his courage, Ratzel called down through the ventilator, "Is there anybody down there?"

At which someone replied, "Yes, it's Jimmy, and I want to see you."

At the same time the door burst open and the two boys found themselves covered by weapons that appeared to their frightened eyes like so many cannons.

One of the gang commenced tying Wolf to a lounge, while the others made Ratzel accompany them to the safe downstairs. Here he was ordered in curt terms and profane language to open the safe and be quick about it.

When Ratzel pretended to be unable to open it, claiming to know nothing about the combination, one of the gang spoke up: "I saw you open it this morning."

The youth fumbled with the dial, still claiming he could not comply with the request, when one fellow pressed the cold end of a weapon behind his ear. Ratzel heard the click caused by the drawing of the hammer. When he saw no other way out, he tried to open the lock, but owning to his nervousness, he failed in his first attempt. He thought his last moment had come, and it would have been so had there been someone else at hand to work the combination.

Finally, however, the door opened. The haul the gang made was apparently much more than expected. This fact may have saved Ratzel's life. The exact amount of the take could never be ascertained, though it is said to have been about $2,000.

After rifling the safe, the bandits took Ratzel upstairs and tied him to the posts of his bed. His watch, which they at first wanted to take, was returned to him.

Before departing, the bandits warned the boys to keep quiet and not to make any noise, assuring them that one of the gang would be about and would promptly "fix" them in case they disobeyed orders.

The gang drove to Marengo and, with the exception of the Green brothers, took the early morning passenger train. Conductor Rainor, who had charge of the train, noticed their drenched clothing, but only several days later when he heard of the robbery did he suspect the party and connect them with the crime.

Ratzel, after about an hour of twisting and pulling, finally succeeded in getting free, on which he liberated Wolf and aroused the town.

The Green brothers were apprehended a few months later when they tried to sell some of the purloined stamps. They confessed their guilt and through them it became known that Jesse James himself had participated in this raid.

The Green brothers were imprisoned for a number of years, but James and his gang continued free.

Wolf suffered from nervousness for a long time when he had to continue to sleep in the same room. He later left with a relative from Illinois, but returned to the Amanas in later years and died in 1927.

Editor's note:There was no doubt the store was robbed. Some historians question if the robbers were the Jesse James gang, however, the whereabouts of Jesse James was unknown during the year 1877.

Spring Tours

Cedar Rapids Gazette, May 1, 1884

A May party left the city this morning for the Amanas under the direction of Superintendent Earling of the C.M.&St.P. Railway. Mayor Eaton, Treasurer Stoddard, besides several aldermen and citizens went with the party, who are off for an excursion and tour of inspection, and if they like the colonies and the Milwaukee road, will buy them outright. The party returns promptly at eight o'clock tonight, even if this is Bock Beer Day.

The Amana Trip

Cedar Rapids Gazette, May 29, 1884

Something in regard to the society not generally known—but yet of interest.

The Methodist excursion of Amana has come and gone, and it was voted by one and all a great success. Everything passed off quietly and peacefully, and financially it went well also.

Bro. Dorwart is a "dandy" indeed. He managed the affair and a vote of thanks is due him except for two things: one, because the excursionists could not get to South Amana, but for which he was not to blame, and because they were compelled to wait until 7:45, the regular train time, to get home.

But what of Amana?

There are few people who have a good idea of Amana, and fewer who realize the working of the institution. It is remarkable in its management and character and furnished food for a vast amount of thought. A few observations made for the benefit of our readers and, taken from life, may be of interest.

The society is composed of about fifteen hundred people, and they own twenty-seven thousand acres of as fine a land as lies outdoors. It was established in 1854 by some gentlemen who came from the Ebeneezer society of New York, as we understand it. And we might say here that we are liable to make some errors in this article because of the difficulty experienced in getting the facts regarding any of the important matters. One of the gentlemen would explain a thing and another would give altogether a different idea of it. But the Amana Society was organized about thirty years ago, at a time when land was exceedingly cheap, and they entered many quarter sections from the government as low as $1.25 per acre. They have seven villages, five on the north side of the Iowa River called East Amana, Amana proper, Middle Amana, Upper Amana and West Amana. On the south side of the river the largest town is Homestead, on the C.R.I.&P. railway where President Marshall resides and where they have their wholesale stores. South Amana, also located on the C.R.I.&P. Railway is five miles south of Homestead and the C.M.&St.P. railroad have reached that point. Each village contains its own stores, blacksmith shops, watchmakers and mechanics in general, where all the work of one particular kind is done, not only for themselves but for the surrounding country. The society is a regular organization having a constitution and by-laws and is based upon the one idea of Christian principle— evangelical in faith. They don't take any of the Fathers Luther, John Husk, Knox or Wesley as their leader, and have no paid priestcraft, but simply have faith in the Holy Ghost somewhat on the Quaker order, and the only thing they have in the way of preaching is through their elders, who, if moved by the spirit, get up and exhort. They have nightly prayer meetings, where, while there is no compulsion about it, all are expected to attend.

They have a large meetinghouse in each village where they hold services, and they don't call it church. Beneath the meetinghouses are their large, well-filled wine cellars, in which altogether they have over 50,000 gallons stored.

"There's a spirit above and a spirit below —
A spirit of love and a spirit of woe
The spirit above is the spirit Divine,
The spirit below is the spirit of wine."

Each village has a vineyard of from five to seven acres, and the vintage of 1883 produced 2,700 gallons at Amana proper, fronting on the northwest side of a lake that contains nearly one hundred acres and is from ten to twenty feet deep.

The president is the chief officer, elected for life, and he has a board of thirteen trustees. There are no houses scattered over their land, but all reside in these seven villages as named. There are no separate families, but they have kitchens, so called, where a certain number take their meals, several families living in one house and all go out to these kitchens for their meals. In each department there is a "boss" who directs the work from day to day. He reports to the president and is responsible to him for the proper management of his department. Nobody draws a salary, but each has an allowance for wearing apparel, and we understand that the gentlemen are allowed $30 per year for their clothing. The children have provision made for them also, according to the number in the family. No one can draw out money unless permitted by the trustees for traveling expenses in case they wish to visit outside of the society.

To join the institute requires one to subscribe to their religious doctrine, and to perform manual labor when in health. They are not given a certain amount of work to do, but go at it slowly and leisurely. In case a person joins the society and puts money therein, he may take it out without interest any time he becomes dissatisfied. His capital does not increase, but he gets his living the same as others. Young men or girls born in the society are permitted to leave at any time with a certain amount of money to try the ways of the outside world, and at any time when they become dissatisfied they may return. This has been demonstrated in this city by several servant girls and mechanics, the former earning from $2 to $3 per week and the latter $1.75 to $2 per day. Most of them remained away from the society from six months to a year and returned to the society disgusted with the ways of the world.

We shall tomorrow give further details of the workings of the society and many important items that will no doubt be of interest to our readers, and the article may possibly continue the next day also.

The excursionists, of whom there were about one hundred and seventy-five, returned at 9 o'clock last night, having had an enjoyable time and learned a good deal.

Life in the Amana Colony

Chautauqua, Vol. 8. October-July 1887-1888
By Albert Shaw, Ph.D.

The cooperative village, with diversified industries based upon agriculture as the main industry, has been the ideal of many social reformers and is still the fond anticipation of not a few practical men. The organization of industry and the domestic economy of a communistic society whose basis is agriculture, yet whose industrial life is varied and so far as possible complete within itself, may bear very importantly upon the question of whether purely cooperative village life could be made feasible and profitable. Every trace of communism might be eliminated from the constitution of a society like Amana and cooperation substituted therefore, without visibly affecting the mechanism of social and industrial life. So radical a change in the motif of the association, which is held together by a peculiar religious creed, might cause rapid disintegration. But in outward form Amana is a miniature cooperative commonwealth, and some account of its structure and arrangements may be permitted, especially in view of the fact that from the standpoint of cooperation this particular society is by far the most important of the communist groups of the country.

The purpose of this sketch forbids a detailed account of the industries of the Amana colony, but they may be briefly described. Most important are the two large woolen mills, one in the central village and the other Middle Amana. The yarns and flannels of these mills are not surpassed, and are in demand everywhere in the country. The annual output is said to be worth about half a million dollars. The operatives are all men, and a majority of them are past middle life. They are as hale and interesting a body of old men as can be found anywhere. Long practice has given them great skills. They have a fine pride in the perfection of their goods, and quality is their first object. The factories are supplied with excellent machinery. Everybody in them is industrious and cheerful, while nobody is overworked. I do not believe that so intelligent and well-conditioned a group of operatives can be found in any other factories on earth.

This incomplete sketch must of necessity leave unsaid very many things that should have place in a full description of life at Amana. It is a community in which crime is absolutely unknown. In deference to the laws and institutions of the state, the colonists go through the form of electing a justice of the peace and a constable for their township, but these officers have nothing to do. Pauperism, of course, is a term that has no meaning in a communistic society. The even and wholesome life of the colony is conducive to good health and great longevity. If there are vicious and ill-disposed persons in the colony, I have seen none of them and have heard of none. I mean, of course, such persons as would be regarded in any good community as bad members of society. I have seen in the colony no faces that excited distrust and dislike. The life is unquestionably promotive of moral excellence. The average of physical comfort is high, but it might easily be higher. The wants of the people are few and simple, and they do not aspire to "all the modern conveniences." Their intellectual standard also is low. They might have libraries and reading rooms and a central high school with the best appliances, but this is not what they want. They live under the restriction of a narrow creed. Obviously their life has its unfavorable as well as its favorable side. There have been troubles and disagreements at times, undoubtedly. As society at large is now constituted, nothing could be more hopelessly impractical, for general adoption, than the communistic program. But there is much in a community like Amana to strengthen faith in the feasibility of cooperation.

Woolen Mill and Flour Mill

71

Excerpts from

Picturesque Amana: A Sketch

Interesting Pen Picture of Iowa's Greatest "Colony" With Some Characteristic Views-Most Popular of All Spots for Cedar Rapids Excursionists

Cedar Rapids Gazette, January 9, 1904
By B. L. Wick

About twenty miles southwest of Cedar Rapids, in Iowa county, can be found what is known as the "Dutch Colony," in history called "Community of True Inspiration," and in law, for it is a corporation, "The Amana Society." It is a place worthy of study for to it come annually from all parts of the country investigators and historians to study its workings, its plans, and its conditions.

Of the hundreds of communistic societies which have been organized in this country in the past fifty years, this is the only one which can show from the beginning to the present time an increase in wealth and membership....

Workings of the Society

In spite of the fact that they have existed in America as a society for sixty years, the visitor finds strong traces of the old German ideals. Seven villages comprise this little Germany in Iowa. As one saunters up and down the long winding street there can be heard no gossip, no noise, and no storytelling on store boxes as one finds in so many of the small towns. The people go back and forth from work, greet one another cordially and pass on, each one having some one thing to do, and go about doing it. It makes no difference if the members be old or young; the work best suited for them is prepared, and part of the day, at least, is devoted to work by all ablebodied members. There are no drones here, and hence perhaps we have the evidence of prosperity and contentedness.

It is Tolstoy who claims that if all the able-bodied persons worked, the average time each one would need to work would be about five hours per day—that is this large percentage of the non-working classes which makes the long hours. This I believe is true, at least to a certain extent, for among the members of the society engaged in farm work, for instance, it is done with less friction and with less waste of nerve energy than on the adjoining farms, for here there is a system; every able-bodied person has some part of the work planned for him to do, it is done in time, and there is no overwork, and this is one of the charms of communism—to make work pleasant and not drudgery. In the colony the work is shifted so that the factory help in summer is used on the farm and the farm help of the summer help in winter and fall in the factory. Thus it can be seen that the inside workers can have an outing and at the same time be of material value to the community during a season of the year when work inside would be trying, and at a time when farm help would be nearly impossible to obtain. Everyone knows that much time is wasted by the farmers during this season in order to obtain help. This is done away with in the colony. When the colonists do hire help, they pay generally about $10 per month less on account of fewer hours actually engaged in labor.

No Hard Times Here

In traveling about the county during flush and hard times, one is struck with the squallor on one hand and the waste on the other. Such a condition does not exist in the community where there are neither flush times nor hard times. Here they go about the even tenor of their ways regardless of crop failures, steel trust combinations, wheat corners or the like. They pay cash for what they purchase; close the factories when sales are light, and only work to the full capacity when trade is brisk. Whether this could be carried out on a large scale may be doubted, and is even so looked upon by the directors of the society.

The reason that this communistic scheme was adopted was on account of the poverty of so many members, whose conditions might be improved if this method was carried out, making all equal. This meant a great deal to the settlers at that time, when we remember that it was not only sharing one another's religious views, but their hard-earned money as well. It seems that the wealthy were as willing to place thousands into the common fund as the poor were willing to put in a few dollars, the only provision being that when a member left the community he was entitled to the original sum paid in, without interest and without compensation for time spent working for the society.

Others Succeed Less

The question arises: what could other emigrants have accomplished if they had taken up some phases of communism? What could the Hollanders have accomplished, or the thousands of expeditions sent to this country from Scandinavia, Ireland, Scotland, Germany and Bohemia?

They could have worked and saved, and have considerable to show for the labor expended, but much has been done at great expense and after many tribulations. They may not have been richer in money but one thing is certain, they could have had more of the comforts of life, more of its pleasures, had they helped one another during the early years of their travels from place to place in America in search of homes. The communities have succeeded best where they have united together in localities having some of the community features, such as schools, churches, a common tongue and where the leaders of the communities have looked after those less fortunate and less progressive. In these foreign settlements there is always found in each place several leaders who are consulted in matters of various kinds. Such men have been of great value and deserve much more praise and higher honor than they generally receive for the interest they took in their less fortunate countrymen, ignorant of the language and of the laws of their adopted county.

One of the reasons for the success of the Amana Society has been their conception of communism and their Teutonic mode of local self-government. It has been ascertained time and time again, that the success of such an experiment does not depend so much upon the learning of the individual members, as upon the shrewdness and good common sense of its officers and its members. Society must know that we are not all equal. One is born to leadership, while another can only succeed as a servant or in doing the biddings of his superior. These people have early put this in practice, and they have always had very competent men as leaders in business matters, who have directed affairs where the others followed willingly, and those less competent were just as essential to the success of the experiment by displaying the other qualities, viz.: industry, frugality and perseverance.

Another reason for their success is the use of the German tongue, which has bound the members together. Indeed it has been often said that a common origin, a common tongue and a common religion are the three most powerful concomitants of national life, and the same rule applies when applied to a small community like the Amana Society; where men and women associate together, whose aims, beliefs and principles are identical.

From observations which I have made from time to time, when I have been among them, I have found that they have as much happiness and perhaps more comforts than most of the people outside; they may not have as much freedom, of course. They live well, dress well, are cleanly and have all the comforts found in the average home in America, if not more; the children are given the best educational advantages, and are early taught to labor. If a boy is promising, he is sent away to school to study for a doctor or dentist or some other line, the expense being borne by the society.

Thrift is Encouraged

A colonist does not have money, and still he is never without it, and can order what he needs and the amounts used are deducted from his account. Each member is allowed about $35 per year for spending money, everything else being furnished free. This sum is also frequently left and added to the sum placed to the credit of each individual. Thrift is encouraged, and this is taught in the school and at homes.

The old German home life is encouraged. One family, or at least the one house, and the garden in which they take a great pride, is the individual property. About forty persons eat at the same boarding-house called the "kitchen." In old Amana there are about sixteen of these eating places. In the hamlet of about 550 people they have all the advantages of a great city. There is the butcher, the baker, the iceman, the milkman, the street cleaner, the water supply man, the store, the jeweler, and in fact, every trade and occupation, and still it costs the member absolutely nothing. He has his clothes washed and ironed, his watch repaired, his food and his lodging, all free by only working about seven or eight hours, and an assurance of a comfortable old age with a bank account to the credit of his children at his death.

In Religious Matter

In religious matters eighty elders selected by vote of the society look after all the details of the work, women having the same privileges as the men. They also engage in the ministry.

Are Law Abiding

It has been said that we are a nation of lawbreakers: that we have no scruples about breaking the laws if these are obnoxious to our views. This no doubt engenders the same feeling in children, and so it goes on getting a little worse with every generation. The colonists have still the old-German idea of obeying the law and instill this into their children, not only at home but in the shop and in the school. During the sixty years that this society has existed in this country, I am informed that not a penny has been expended by the state in prosecution of criminal trials against members of the society. Take again, on the other hand as an example, the Jukes, where Mr. Dugdale, the author, states that this degenerate family has cost the state, during the period of seventy five years, more than a million and a half in money to say nothing about the pauperism and crime which this family left for succeeding generations to battle with. I am not arguing that the colonists had the criminal tendencies instinct like the criminal family just referred to. Let me also cite further that these people, a few years ago, closed up their breweries on account of the law enacted in this state by a majority vote. Obeying the law is part of their moral code.

Perfect equality is shown even in death, for if one wanders into the cemetery he will find an absence of family lots and monuments; each grave is marked by a small slab with a simple inscription, and no flowers are displayed. It resembles more the cemetery of a great battlefield with the marks in long rows, "unknown" chiseled on each slab.

However, it has been in just such a cemetery that I have had my doubts about the outcome of communism, and whether it can ever be realized as the only means for a rectification of society. I have sat under the branches of the shade trees and watched a woman dressed in the Amana costume enter the lonely place with a sorrowful face, saw her go to a corner in that lot near a newly made grave and there stand and meditate over the loss of an infant child or a loving father. Perhaps that mourner knew a majority of those who had been laid away in that graveyard, and she no doubt had a kindly feeling for all, like her own great loss, which no amount of sympathy and sorrow on part of the others could remove. It was her own individual loss, which only she in all this world could feel and treasure, such a loss which as

Irving fittingly says: "Where is the mother who would willingly forget the infant that perished like a blossom from her arm, although every recollection is a pang? Where is the child that would willingly forget the most tender of parents, although to remember is but to lament?"

What will be the future of this interesting community in close proximity to thriving cities of this prosperous west? Will they end up in court like the Icarian community in Adams county, which after half a century of communistic life was compelled to say to the world "that there was a long distance from desire to realization, from principle to fact, from theory to practical embodiment?"

Mighty changes are taking place in our American life. There is a social unrest everywhere. Will it penetrate the portals of Amana society? If it does, it may be difficult to predict the outcome. I can only add that the old pioneers who led the little band across the sea, who found homes for their less fortunate brothers, parting with their money in order to realize certain ideals, deserve the highest praise among the thousands of emigrants who have come to our shores. The worthy sons of these honored sires, who by perseverance and force of character, have kept the members of the society together these many years and should not be forgotten in mentioning the builders of Iowa.

Woolen Mill worker 1900s

Life in Amana, Iowa

Dr. Winship Visits Most Famous "Community" of the New World Where 1,800 People Live in Comfort, Peace, Prosperity

The Journal, Somerville, Massachusetts, September 16, 1904
By A.E. Winship

There is one genuinely prosperous, peaceful, and apparently eternal communistic settlement in the New World. I have known at first hand in their prime the other important experiments in communistic life, and have seen them all transformed or altogether put out of commission because of inability to meet local prejudices, legal requirements, or industrial conditions. Hence the satisfaction with which, from time to time, I have studied the Amana settlement, which is apparently as secure as the Hawkeye state, as prosperous as Wall Street, as harmonious as a honeymoon.

There is no more beautiful farm country between the seas than the forty square miles of rolling prairie which the Amana colony owns and occupies. This vast farm has two beautiful lakes, about ten miles of the Iowa River, which winds through its rich fields, and ten square miles of oak, hickory, hemlock, maple, and walnut, so that one never sees fields of oats, corn, wheat, or grass without a rich background of hardwood grove-forest.

Each family has its own home. There is no dash of paint on any building, inside or out, but this is scarcely missed because everything is scrupulously clean. Not a home is without its flowers, fruits, and vegetables; not one is without its large, clean yard, its out-of-door benches and vine-covered arbor. Not a weed peeps out anywhere. Not a family is without its vegetable garden of celery, asparagus, lettuce, radishes, beets, cucumbers, melons, onions, turnips, cauliflower, beans, peas, early potatoes, and early corn.

Every rod of the forty square miles of woods, fields, and gardens is groomed as though it were the pet luxury of some multi-millionaire. There is no fringe of weeds about the cornfield, no underbrush sapping the life of the native forest groves, no seed wafting lusty weeds by the roadside. Nowhere is there a shaky fencepost, a broken rail, a lopped branch of a tree, or weak plank in a bridge. Nowhere is there a neglected bit of farm machinery, or a ragged roadside woodpile.

The barn and barnyard of each village is ideal. All in all, there are 200 noble horses in the colony—large, handsome, well groomed, with fine harnesses and the latest styles of wagons, of which there are 300. There are 1,800 sleek, fat cows, calves, and oxen, 3,500 blooded sheep. All stock is of the best in blood and breed.

The colony has no township officers, as it owns one entire township of thirty-six square miles, and pays no county, road or school tax. It is allowed to build and keep its own roads in repair, and they are the best in the state. They build their own schoolhouses, and the schools are virtually in session fifty-two weeks in the year, getting now and then a day off when the teacher and older pupils are needed at some crisis in the farming, or when the teacher—always a man—has occasion to be away for a day, which is rare. The school day knows no five-hour limit.

There is nothing strenuous about their school life, but without any fuss the children learn German and English, reading and writing them with equal fluency. They all write a clear, plain hand, and know numbers, language, and geography well, but with none of the frills. They all have more or less of industrial school work. The girls, even the littlest girls, knit and sew in schools like artists with the needles.

In dress, customs, and manners they are a simple folk, and in everything scrupulously neat. There is a general sameness in the dress of the women, though it comes from its simplicity and from the fact that the goods are made in the community. There is something of individuality. Every garment is whole, unpatched, and nothing has an overworn look. Thrift marks everything and everybody at Amana. A smile of contentment, a look of comfort characterizes all the women and children, especially.

If there are seeds of discontent, if there is suppressed discord, if elements of ultimate disruption are being nursed, I have never discovered them among the leaders or in the rank and file, and I prophesy the same peace and prosperity of Amana fifty years hence as today.

Is Amana Society in Great Danger?

Much Interest Manifested Here in Action Commenced

**Considerable Speculation as to Who Is Behind
Mrs. Martha Wilson, "The Woman in the Case"
—Many Statements Are Circulated Not Founded on Facts**

Cedar Rapids Gazette, February 8, 1905

Will a woman be able to bring about the dissolution of the Amana Society in Iowa County, the most powerful and likewise the most successful communistic society in the world?

This a question that is proving of the greatest interest to Cedar Rapids people, who are likewise trying to fathom the animus back of the action of Mrs. Martha Wilson, a resident of Iowa County, upon whose complaint Judge Byington has instructed County Attorney Wallace of Iowa County to bring an action to determine whether the society is not going beyond its corporate powers. They are also wondering who are behind the movement besides Mrs. Wilson. There has been much mystery surrounding the action which has been commenced, although it has been intimated that the suit has really been instituted on behalf of dissatisfied members of the society. In fact, there has been more or less intimation of sensational developments, it being the evident intention to surround the matter with as much mystery as possible.

It has evidently been sought to have the impression go forth that the suit has been brought to force payment of taxes, it being intimated that the society, during its half century of existence, has been escaping the payment of its just share of taxes. On the other hand the complainant sets out that the society was incorporated as a religious and benevolent organization under the laws of Iowa, refers to the five or six amendments made to the original constitution from time to time and alleges the society is not now engaged in strictly religious or benevolent enterprises, for it is the owner of two whole townships, of several towns, stores, industries, etc., and that, as a matter of fact, the affairs of the society are being conducted for pecuniary benefit and profit.

At the same time it has been claimed, although this is not set out in the petition, that there is much dissatisfaction among the members of the society and that this action in the courts is but a forerunner of a movement looking toward a disruption of the society. It is said there is the greatest dissatisfaction among the young men of the society. Under the provisions of the constitution of the society, a person withdrawing from it does not receive his proportionate share of the wealth held in trust by the managing members. It is said the younger members want to leave, yet do not care to sacrifice their share of the money involved and are desirous of having the society dissolved, in which event each one would receive some $5,000 or $6,000.

The Amanites came to Iowa in 1855, coming here from New York for the purpose of establishing a communistic society. There were about 500 members of the society at that time and among them some very able men and women. They purchased about 26,000 acres of land in Iowa County, which at that time was on the frontier. Much of the land was secured from the government and for none of it did they pay more than $5 an acre. The 500 people have increased to between 1,800 and 1,900 and the land is today worth from $60 to $100 an acre. The affairs of the colony have not been conducted for pecuniary gain, or with the expectation of acquiring wealth, yet today the society is worth not less than $2,000,000 and it may reach $3,000,000.

For the first few years, the society occupied a peculiar position, existing merely as a partnership. But it became evident that some action was necessary. In the meantime a law had been passed providing for the incorporation of societies for religious, benevolent, and educational purposes, and under this statue, the society incorporated in 1860. While the society was not organized for pecuniary profit, it has always been conceded that it was quite necessary to engage in agricultural and other pursuits for gain for otherwise the life of the colony would be of short duration. Nevertheless, it has always been a question whether the society has been incorporated under the right statute. Attorneys have never felt able to answer the matter one way or the other and the matter heretofore has never been brought into the courts. At the same time it has always been conceded that the society has been conducted along the lines of the original intention, and that there has been no effort at deception or fraud.

There has always been some dissatisfaction among the younger members of the society, and from time to time, both young men and young women have left there to make for themselves a place in the outside world. Their life is so at variance with the rest of the world that this is not at all to be wondered at, for among all classes of people and in all stations of life there are to be found those who are more ambitious than those about them, who are not satisfied with the environments and possibilities. Every person born of members of the society may become members themselves upon attaining a certain age, both male and female, and have an equal voice in determining the affairs of the organization.

Some of the statements given circulation since the commencement of the suit in Iowa County are not founded on facts, showing either a desire to misrepresent or else ignorance of the true state of affairs. One statement is that under the constitution of the colony any member, upon withdrawing therefore, does not receive his proportionate share of wealth held, but is given a sum equal to $25 per year for the number of years he has spent in the colony. This is not true. In the first place, it costs no member of the colony anything for food, clothing, fuel, medicine or any of the necessities of life. In addition to this, each one is given a sum of money equal to about $25 a year for luxuries. No money is used. Each member has a book, which is kept balanced. Each time a purchase is made it is charged up in his individual book. Upon the withdrawal of a member, he receives all that belongs to him individually, without interest, but does not receive any of the undivided profits. For instance, if a member had turned over to the society $500 when he became a member, or had been left that amount by his parents, upon withdrawal he would receive $500, without interest, however, no matter how long it had been used; neither would he receive any share of the undivided profits.

The statement that the colony has not been paying taxes is another erroneous one. *The Gazette* learned that their property has always been assessed and that they have paid their full share of taxes. However, it is interesting to note that the per capita tax of Iowa County, including members of the Amana Society, is not so large as the per capita tax in the surrounding counties, but with the 1,800 or 1,900 Amanites excluded, the per capita tax is about the same as in the surrounding counties. Those in a position to know say that this does not indicate an evasion of taxes by any means, but rather demonstrates the affairs of the colony are not primarily conducted for pecuniary profit, declaring that the accumulation of wealth is incidental to the wise conduct of the affairs of the organization, to the great increase in land values, and to the fact that none of the members live extravagantly or luxuriously.

The people who are members of the Amana colony, it is said by those who have made a study of conditions there, do not work hard. Instead of from ten to eighteen hours a day, as in the outside world, none work more than eight hours a day. It is a noticeable fact that outside help to the farms can be secured for from $12 to $13 a month, while farmers across the line must pay from $20 to $25 a month. This is because they do not work so hard in the colony and live better.

There is another theory for the reason why the per capita tax of Iowa County with the colony included is smaller than in the surrounding counties. Those who have left the society are the younger men and women and the majority of the membership are older people whose earning capacity is less than would be the case if young blood predominated.

Those who live here, who know of the conditions there, declare there is no dissatisfaction among the members more than there has ever been. It is pointed out that the majority rules there and that the matter of making changes has not been brought up. It is also believed that if it shall be decided in the courts that the society has not been incorporated under the proper statue that immediate steps will be taken to re-incorporate under that section which provides for organizations formed for pecuniary profit. The society could then be conducted under the present constitution, but it would be necessary to re-incorporate every twenty years. If this action becomes necessary, it is believed that very few, if any, of the present members would withdraw. Certain it is, not enough would withdraw to embarrass the colony or cause its disruption.

But the county attorney of Iowa County is now preparing the papers, at the insistance of a woman who declares the colony is harmful to society and that it has not been paying its share of taxes. If the matter is carried through, a number of most interesting questions will be solved. As indicated in the dispatches yesterday, the society will make a bitter fight, carrying the matter to the Supreme Court of the United States if necessary. Their defense, it is stated, will be that while they are engaged in ordinary business pursuits as a corporation, it is done for benevolent purposes, the building up of the society.

Fred Oehl, Sr, photographed the people coming from a church service in Amana early 1900s.

The Amana Case Heard in Court

Davenport Democrat, July 23, 1905

The case of Mrs. Wilson vs. the Amana Society, to test its right to corporate existence, was concluded yesterday before Judge Byington, holding court at Marengo, and was taken under advisement by him. The case resembled a Mormon investigation by a senate committee, except that the Amana people were not charged with any crime, social or otherwise, unless, perhaps, it is a crime to own 26,000 acres of the finest land in Iowa, besides untold wealth in manufacturing and milling industries, as is shown the Amana colony owned.

The suit, however, brought out many interesting facts not generally understood, particularly as to the religious belief of these Mennonites. As the defense is that they hold the lands and minister to the affairs of the colony as a religious duty, the testimony as to their belief was particularly explicit. One fact brought out was that Mennonites advocate celibacy, a feature of their religion which is a good deal of a surprise, even to those who have known them for years. They hold that a bachelor is on a higher plane spiritually than his married brother, and that he has a better chance of getting through the pearly gates.

George Heinemann, one of the elders of the society,...testified to this. He said, however, that their religious belief did not forbid marriage....they recognized the necessity for it. To quote the witness: "It is good to be married, but it is better to be single." This, they say, was taught by the Apostle Paul. Spiritually, the members of the society are divided into three classes. A single man is in the first class, and if he marries he drops to the third. The testimony did not bring out the nature of the second class. When a man marries he does not lose social prestige or any of this civil rights; he is simply a loser spiritually. The trimming of the beard differentiates the three classes. Mr. Heinemann brought out that the holding of property in common was part of their religious belief, and his evidence on this point is expected to have a large bearing on the issue of the case. He said that they held property in common in order that the members might be free from the ordinary cares and worries of life, and devote themselves to spiritual things.

Iowa Supreme Court May Dissolve Amana Society

Attorneys Arguing Today to Break Up Largest Communistic Society in the World

Des Moines Register, June 3, 1906

Can a religious society attempting to obey the injunction of the apostle to have all property in common, exist legally under the laws of Iowa and own thousands of acres of land and millions of dollars of property and do a business reaching nearly a million of dollars a year? This is the question that has been submitted to the Supreme Court of Iowa in the case of the State vs. the Amana Society.

The Amana Society, a peculiar religious organization of Iowa County, claims it has a right to do business for profit the same as any business concern, but escapes taxation because it is a religious society and attempting to obey the apostle's orders to have all things in common. The state of Iowa, through Attorney General Mullan, asserted before the Supreme Court today that the society may carry out its religious desires and live with all things in common, but that it must incorporate as any other concern for pecuniary profit must incorporate.

The courts are asked to dissolve the society by appointing a receiver and distributing the property to the members of the society unless it incorporates.

The magnitude of the questions before the Iowa Supreme Court is best understood in the inventory in the printed argument of Attorney General Mullan and in his oral arguments made to the Supreme Court today. The Amana Society was incorporated as a religious organization December 1, 1859, and its corporate existence has been extended from time to time. Here are the leading facts concerning it:

Land: 26,225 acres in Iowa and Johnson counties of the average value of $40; total, $1,049,000. Under cultivation, 5,386 acres; meadow and pasture, 7,026; uncultivated, 13,713.

Industries: Two woolen factories, one cotton print factory, four hotels, seven general stores, three drugstores, seven blacksmiths, three lumberyards, coal and lime yards.

Population: 7 villages, 280 dwellings, 51 barns, 1,000 members.

Annual products of the society reach nearly a million dollars, and those that are sold on the market and not consumed by the society reach over a half-million of dollars and are as follows:

Merchandise from stores	$136,000
Woolen products	145,000
Cotton mill products	70,000
Flouring mill products	76,000
Livestock sold	123,000
Total.	$550,000

Attorney General Mullan argued before the Supreme Court today in the case that the society has exceeded its powers under its articles of incorporation as a religious society and that by that act its charter has been forfeited. He argued that whatever the religious beliefs of the 1,000 or more members of the society as to living with all property in common the society had, in fact, become a gigantic corporation doing a business amounting to an immense profit each year and that whenever a religious society attempts to obtain property and wealth and power through secular business, it transcends the authority conferred upon it by the state, and the fact that members claim that the transaction of such business and the gaining of such wealth is a part of the religious beliefs of the society is no answer to the charge made by the state that it is violating the laws by which it was created.

The possibility that the society may some day become as menacing as the Mormon Church is suggested by Attorney General Mullan in his argument today. He said: "It is true that the Amana Society has not attempted to acquire the temporal power which was attained by the Mormon Church, but can it be said that in the future some strong ambitious man actuated by a desire to extend the influence of the society and to greatly increase its wealth and property may not become the head and ruling spirit of the corporation? If that should occur, and it is held that the society may, under its articles of incorporation, transact all classes of secular business as a part of its religious belief, no reason exists why, under the management of such an ambitious head, the society may not extend its influence over a large portion of the state, and hold in its own right, many hundred thousand acres of land, and thereby become a dominate power which will be partially beyond the control of the courts and state authorities. The suggestion is not exaggerated. The prototype exists in the Mormon Church."

The attorneys for the society, led by Judge M.J. Wade of Iowa City, maintain that the articles of incorporation and by-laws of the society give it authority to transact this business. Attorney General Mullan claims that the articles may state that authority, but the articles can only exist under the law and the law does not allow religious societies to have such powers. The attorney for the society claims the rights under the United States constitution which guarantees religious liberty. The attorney for the state argues that public policy demands that religious societies shall not have authority to engage in secular pursuits since "such societies discourage individual effort, the building of homes and the rearing of families in those homes. So far as their influence goes, the tendency is to remove the very foundation stone upon which our society rests, the individual home."

Oxen plowed the prairie and were worked well into the 20th century. Each of the seven villages was an hour apart by ox cart. Photo 1900s.

Amana Society Wins Its Case

Iowa Supreme Court Hands Down Important Decision
Holds That Society Is Not Organized and Conducted for
Financial Gain—Religion Defined

Cedar Rapids Gazette, November 21, 1906

Definition of religion and discussion of what constitutes a religious society constitute an important and interesting part of a decision which was handed down by the Iowa Supreme Court yesterday in which the standing of the Amana Society as a religious community is vindicated, and the decision of the lower court dismissing the action praying the dissolution of the corporation and the forfeiture of the privileges enjoyed by it as such is affirmed.

The case came from Iowa County, where it was tried before Judge O.A. Byington about a year ago. It was brought by the state of Iowa on complaint of Martha Wilson, who alleged that, though incorporated as a religious organization, the society, in violation of its charter rights, engaged in agricultural enterprises for financial gain.

The questions chiefly confronting the supreme court were: First, "What is religion?" and second, "Is the property of this society used for religious purposes?"

Religion Defined

The attorney general, in presenting his arrangement on the appeal from the lower court, laid down the issue fairly in his definition of religion. He says: "Religion pertains to the spiritual belief and welfare of man" as distinct from his physical wants and necessities. It relates to the ethics of life, to hope and a belief in immortality.

"Secular pursuits, on the other hand, are those pertaining to the material and physical wants of man and are clearly distinct from holy interests: not immediately or primarily respecting the soul, but the body."

The attorney general based his argument on this ground, to the effect that the Amana Society was not purely a religious body, as incorporated.

In its answer to this definition the decision of the court says that while the statement of the attorney general may perhaps be theoretically correct, the practical and religious cannot be so easily divorced in everyday life.

Creeds Depend Upon Followers

"The anticipated advantages of nearly every religion or creed are made dependent on the life its followers live and the criticisms oftenest heard are that the exalted doctrines of righteousness professed are too frequently forgotten in the ordinary pursuits of life and that the contests for wealth, in some circles, are waged with the raspicity of beasts of prey. Surely a scheme of life designed to obviate such results and, by removing temptation and all inducements of ambition and avarice, to nurture the virtues of unselfishness, patience, love and service ought not to be denounced as not pertaining to religion when its devotees regard it as an essential tenet of their religious faith.

"The court holds that the Amana Society is founded for such a purpose as outlined, finds that no speculation is permitted in its real estate transactions, and that there is no effort to secure an income greater than the needs of the organization.

"It discounts the argument that such a communal settlement is dangerous to American ideals and politics and, in conclusion, holds that the society has not exceeded its powers as a religious corporation and affirms the decision of the lower court."

The Hahn family group, Middle Amana 1900s

Excerpts from

An Arcadia in America

Practicing the Gospel of Work, the Amana Society Has Actually Realized the Dream of the Political Theorist

The Home Magazine, 1906
By Viola Gardner Brown

The dream, curiously enough, so vainly indulged in by poets and painters of an Arcadian Paradise has been realized by a people who have been associated together for two centuries, yet who, paradoxical as it may seem, never dream. The only communistic society that has been at all successful or survived for any considerable length of time is the "Society of the True Inspiration," the church name of the Amana Community in Iowa. The meaning of the word Amana is "Remain True."

Their belief is similar to the Quakers, and they affirm instead of taking oath, speak in meetings only "when moved by the spirit," and abhor war and litigation....

Property is owned in common, as that plan was adopted in the beginning as the only means of caring for their many converts, poor in all things but the love of God and faith in the new belief. In consequence, there are no rich and no poor, but all are on a perfect equality in all things. When one joins the society, credit is given on the books for what the party brings, and if for any reason he withdraws it is returned without interest.

The fundamental principle of their religion is absolute purity of life. Their churches, of which there is one in each of the seven villages, are very plainly furnished. The wooden seats have backs, but are uncushioned, and the well-scoured floors are bare. There is no pulpit, for there is no preacher, the services being conducted by the eldermen in turn, who rise in their seats and speak. Men and women sit on opposite sides of the room, the elders and most saintly-minded occupying the front seats. The meeting begins with silent prayer, followed by a hymn without accompaniment, as there are no musical instruments in the entire colony. A chapter is read from the Bible, or from the works of one of their inspired writers, of whom they have had several, but none now living. All speak "when the spirit moves them," and they close with another hymn. These services are held on Sundays and on Wednesday nights. There is a brief prayer-meeting every night and, though attendance is not compulsory, all members attend services regularly, rarely missing a night, except for sickness. There are no saloons tolerated in the Amana Society, though they make a superior wine. They do not sell any, and a limited amount is allotted to each family—never enough to permit of any excess.

It is a bit curious that in the Amana Society, as with some other deeply religious organizations, though adhering to a remarkable degree to the teachings of the Bible, especially those of the Old Testament, musical instruments are forbidden, not only in the church services, but throughout the community. It would seem that the very frequent references, especially in the Psalms, to the various musical instruments that were used by the Jews would at least establish the fact that musical instruments were an important part of the religious services, and in some places in the Old Testament minute directions are given as to the style of instruments to be used, as well as the music to be rendered thereon....

The women wear the German peasant dress of two hundred years ago, consisting in summer of a dark calico dress and gingham or calico apron and a light-colored, nearly white, sunbonnet made after a pattern of their own. In cooler weather woolen shoulder shawls are worn, and in winter black hoods. All girls and women wear a little skull cap tied under the chin, which is not removed even when bonnet or hood is worn. This headdress cannot be said to add to their attractiveness, but pride in dress is a thing unknown in the community. There are no milliners or dressmakers, for everyone wears the same garb. The men who work in stores and offices dress like Americans, but the laborers wear the ordinary German peasant clothes.

There are few disagreements of any kind, and if two people have a misunderstanding which promises to be serious, they are "talked to" by the eldermen, and the offender is required to ask pardon. In extreme cases, the belligerents are sentenced to remain away from church for a meeting or two, a punishment that always subdues them...

The Amana people have no social life in the sense in which

Americans use the term. They have no parties, entertainments or amusements of any kind, not even church socials. Cards or games are unknown, and there is nothing to vary the routine of everyday work and church attendance. There is no social intercourse between the sexes, and all work very hard. Every moment of time is improved by young and old. No laughter or loud talking is ever heard, and even the children take life seriously. Passersby never see the little tots playing, but if one is interested to notice, they may see in summertime, out of school hours, the small children at work in the garden, or, if too small for such occupation, the little girls will be sitting in the shade sewing carpet rags or piecing quilts, while the small boys will be seen knitting as they walk about.

There is a strange similarity in the faces of the Amana people. They look like members of the same family, which they are in a sense, having intermarried for two hundred years. Yet some very pretty faces are seen. The young girls have perfect peach-bloom complexions, which the ugly sunbonnets protect from sun and wind. They have an expression of infantile innocence, and in many cases a strange apathetic look. There does not seem to be anything for them to think about, as there is nothing to do but work, and that is all planned for them. Their beauty fades early, strange to say, for their quiet life, according to all accepted belief, should preserve their bloom, but it does not. A few handsome middle-aged women are seen; occasionally one with the face of a saint, but the old women are withered and ugly, perhaps from the life of hard work, with no relaxation or diversion of any kind.

But so sturdy and strong are these people in body, so sincere, earnest and serious-minded, that personal beauty or adornment in no way appeals to them. Beauty in face or figure is of no consideration. They look forward to the end of life complacently and with no misgivings.

If one asks nothing of life but serenity and peace, the Amana Society is the place to live. There are no heart-burnings there, no disappointed ambitions; and while there are hearts, they are carefully kept free from the fancies of a fickle world.

The Amana Community

American Communities and Cooperative Colonies, 1908

By William Alfred Hinds, Ph.D.

Of existing Communistic Societies, Amana has the largest membership, the highest commercial rating for wealth and credit (AAA I), the best prospect of permanency.

Amana is a great example of Communism. More than seventeen hundred people here live in comfort and happiness, each one sure of enough to eat and drink and wear so long as he lives—sure, too, of a home and friends—sure, also, of such discipline and instruction as shall keep him constantly reminded of the supreme importance of a temperate, virtuous holy life. They live in such perpetual peace that no lawyer is found in their midst; in such habits of morality that no sheriff walks their streets; in such plenty that no beggars are seen save such as come from the outer world.

But with all its numbers and wealth, morality and religion, peace and plenty, Amana in many respects fails to realize the blessings which belong to Communism. Knowing full well that "if to do were as easy as to know what were good to do, chapels had been churches, and poor men's cottages princes' places," and every communistic experience a grand success, I will yet mention some of the improvements in Amana's conditions that suggest themselves as within reach:

Every village should have a public library and reading room, where the best books of the outside world are accessible to all the members.

Every village should have a common laundry, with its washing machines and wringers and mangler run by power.

Every village should have large houses in close juxtaposition, all heated by steam and furnished with every labor-saving convenience, instead of its present scores of widely-scattered dwellings. A single kitchen and dining room for each village would then answer in place of the numerous eating houses and save much labor and expense.

Every village should have a public park, beautified with ornamental shade trees, winding paths, grottos and fountains, flower gardens and playgrounds.

Every village should have its musical organization, and all harmless amusements should be encouraged.

The streets and roads and sidewalks should be greatly improved.

The love of the beautiful in nature and art should be encouraged. Now architectural monotony, the entire absence of paint, rough board fences, untidy sidewalks, and other similar features, are everywhere conspicuous in the Amana villages.

The interior of the houses is scarcely more pleasing. There is no ornamentation by paint or paper, carpets or pictures. Everything is plain. Their churches and assembly rooms have only long wooden benches for seats.

Their worship, too, has in it little that is enlivening—much, however that savors of sincerity and earnest piety, and for which unquestionably the members derive inward comfort and strength. But the exercises contrast unfavorably with the spontaneity and freedom which characterize the meetings of some other communistic societies.

Far be it from me to speak disrespectfully of anything in the outward or inward life of this God-fearing people. I fully realize that even such improvements as I have indicated above must be work of years, and this it is for them to determine whether they can ever be safely and wisely made. Their present environments and mode of life are in accordance with their fundamental idea and justified by it, namely, that people are placed in this world for the one purpose of saving their souls, and that this requires the crucifixion of such desires and appetites as divert the attention from God.

Excerpts from

Red and Yellow Wine Poured Into the Street Gutters

All Seven Amana Villages Have Abolished Booze

Cedar Rapids Republican, June 24. 1917

President George Heinemann of the Amana Society, the famous communistic settlement located six miles east of here, has voluntarily presented himself before County Attorney M. Dean Roller and announced that the Amana wine cellars had been abolished and all the wine poured into the gutters.

Mr. Heinemann stated on behalf of the 3,000 colonists he represents that fermented liquor of any kind in the territory occupied by the society would hereafter be confiscated and destroyed wherever found and the laws of the state regarding the use of alcoholic liquors obeyed as explicitly as the Amana authorities could enforce them.

> *"This is the forest primeval,*
> *The murmuring pines and the hemlocks,*
> *Bearded with moss, and in garments green*
> *Indistinct in the twilight*
> *Stand like druids of old."*

"In the ancient city of Eleusis in Attica, many centuries before Christ, there dwelt a famous cult, who have no parallel among ancient religions—so serenely happy in their worship, so remarkably content in their faith and so notoriously constant in their gods that their fame spread over many lands and their beautiful faith gave rise to the expression everywhere common in ancient Greece, "Everyone is happy at Eleusinean.""

The creed of this strange sect not only embraced all the high ideals advocated by early Christian writers, but contained the germ and flower of purest religion. Most sacred and impressive in character were the "Eleusinian Mysteries," the annual ceremony at which hundreds of youths and maidens "pure in heart and not conscious of any crime" were, after months of spiritual meditation, initiated into the coveted organization.

An annual pilgrimage was made from Athens and other Grecian cities to witness this splendid spectacle at the shrine of Apollo on the eastern slope of the Acropolis of Eleusis. Because the site overlooked plains of amazing fertility, the gods were said to have smiled more tenderly upon this spot than anywhere else in Greece. In his admiration for the society, Roger Bacon said of them in his day, "On Christian virtues of faith, hope and charity, we can speak of things of which they knew nothing, but in the virtues needed for integrity of life and for human fellowship, we are not their equals either in word or deed."

Scarcely credible as it may seem, there exists today a counterpart of that Eleusis of old embracing those same characteristics which caused all Greece to marvel, and in addition boasts of many extraordinary distinguishing features unknown to the ancient cult of Eleusis.

The Iowa River, in wending its way through southeastern Iowa, at one particular point sharply changes its course from east to south and thence flows direct to join the Mississippi. Just above the turn, the valley of the historic river discloses a cycle of seven quaint villages slumbering peacefully on the hillsides, the nucleus of a little province embracing 26,000 acres of the richest soil, the choicest natural resources and the most picturesque scenery in Iowa—the seat of Amana, the Community of True Inspiration....

...After a long search for the promised land...their eyes at last were rewarded by the sight of a wonderland so enchanting and alluring they at once realized that the divine prophecy was to be fulfilled in the picturesque garden spot before them. Luxuriant forests and bountiful quarries of sandstone and limestone contributed the choicest of their store toward the material realization of this modern Acadia, the Utopia of Communism and the only successful communistic settlement of forty-nine similar experiments in the history of the United States.

There is no other communistic settlement in America today, similar in character, which has not failed or is failing, few having even existed over a period of eight years.... The Amana of half a century ago is the Amana of today, for the Community of True Inspiration has passed a peaceful, existence marked by few incidents of particular moment. Prosperity has ever-smiled in the little community whose population has doubled and whose wealth has multiplied many times.

...The colonists' uniformly calm and placid features tell the story of their noble lives and testify to the religious prosperity they have enjoyed. Their material prosperity is evidenced in field, factory, orchard, vineyard and garden, but this they consider as secondary and subservient to their chief aim and purpose in life—the purification and sanctification of their souls.

The traveler who has crossed the boundary lines of Amana for the first time is at once charmed by the indescribable sense of peace and quiet which seems to reflect the spirit of the countryside. As he journeys farther in this simple paradise, he may perchance meet a merry group of sweet-faced maidens, singing and chattering in their German tongue, all similarly garbed in the quaint costume of the German peasant of 200 years ago—a picture to linger long in the memory. Flowers and foliage are everywhere in sight, while each turn of the moss-bordered footpath discloses some partially hidden wonder of nature.

Wending his way along the edge of the placid Lake Amana, the stranger must presently find himself at Amana, the capital and largest settlement in the province. He is surprised at the uniform similarity of the massive brown stone houses whose appearance would indeed be monotonous were it not relieved by the profusion of foliage, flowers and trailing vines which everywhere abound.

As the busy hum of yonder factory ceases its labor for the day, a stream of sturdy brethren emerges from its doors, and leisurely wend its way toward the little church for the regular evening prayer meeting. From the houses and gardens, sweet-faced women issue to join the procession, which gradually increases until it embraces the entire population of the village. Sweetly the notes of the vesper bell ring out, echoing over the peaceful lake below, calling the stragglers from the field to forsake their ox teams until the morrow, that the God who has so blessed and sanctified their lives may be glorified; and taking their way over the hillside, they softly chant their beautiful "Evening Song," a sense of indescribable peace and content possessing their hearts, which to the uncomprehending world has been a source of awe and admiration for over half a century.

Editor's note: An Amana joke, at the time, claimed all the fish in Price Creek developed "hangovers."

Put the Colony Out

Marengo Sentinel, March 26, 1918
Reprinted from the *Rock Island* (Illinois) *News*

The *News* has been collecting information in regard to the Amana, Iowa Colony for some time past. This colony has been in existence for over 50 years. Almost actual slavery existed up until a few years ago. Except for corporal punishment, the slavery was as degrading as that of the Negro in the south before the Civil War. They were given practically no education and what little they did get was given in German.

The people are ignorant of the world and as to their rights under the laws of the state. The people have been given no knowledge of any lawful authority other than the head men of the colony. Their word was law and the only law known in the colony. State officials have been slack in their duty for years in regard to school laws and other matters. It is only in recent years that people knew they could leave the colony when they desired without being brought back. Being ignorant of the laws and their rights thereunder, whenever they do leave they are forced to sign a release to the colony that he or she could never claim anything from the colony for wages, etc.

All who have left there have signed these releases, not voluntarily but because they believe they could not leave until they did sign them. The people have never received wages. All they have ever obtained for their labor was their board and clothing, and a house to live in. (The Negro slaves got that much.) The only money they have been able to obtain was by selling some portions of their food or wine to some of the farmers outside the colony.

The leaders have built up an immense fortune in lands, mills, etc., out of the people's labor. Under the law, those people being ignorant of their rights could not legally sign away those rights. The signing of those releases constitutes an act of fraud and misrepresentation, and can be invalidated by action of the courts. Every man and woman whose labor produced that wealth should be given their legal portion of that wealth. As for claiming an exemption on account of religion, that cannot be sustained by the facts in the premises. While they have churches and lay claim to being of the German Lutheran church, yet they have never had any ministers, there has been no preaching, simply a talk and the reading from a little German bible by the leaders. There is no election of leaders in church or colony. Until the last three or four years there were not any English school books in the colony. Their teachers could not pass an examination sufficient to enter as a scholar in the third grade of our public schools.

As an example is one case of a girl now living in Davenport who was hard of hearing, but was desirous of learning in the school. Sometimes in the class not hearing when it came her turn to read, she was passed by by the teacher's order. After a while, on learning that she had been missed in the class, she would ask the teacher: "When do I get to read?" The teacher would then take her book away from her and give her a shingle he kept for that purpose, remarking: "That is good enough for a book for you."

The desire of the leaders seemed to be to keep the people as ignorant as possible, so they could the more easily be kept in slavery. The leaders today are protesting that they are loyal to the United States, while as a matter of fact they are not. They are as much German as if they were actually on German soil. While the local leaders are nominally the heads of the colony, there is every reason existing to cause one to believe that the real owners and supreme leaders are on German soil. The United States government should investigate this colony closely and the actual leaders found. Indications point to the German government being back of the colony.

The colony is a menace to the peace of the state in another way. The morals of the colony are very low. Their system of punishment for immorality actually operates to increase the immorality instead of reducing it.

The church gathering each Sunday is used as a test of good behavior. If one is in bad with the leaders, he or she is forbidden to go to church for many weeks. One is considered in dire disgrace and the whole family of the culprit is considered somewhat disgraced when one of the family is forbidden to attend the weekly meeting.

(We have been told by former members of the Amana Society that the "church" punishment referred to above is meted out to the married women of the colony for the "offense" of producing legitimate

offspring. If that be a fact, then the colony leaders are encouraging race suicide as well as enslaving its members. Be that as it may, read on.—Ed. Sentinel)

Marriage must be by permission of the leaders. When a girl becomes a mother before marriage, and she and the boy desire to marry, under the rules they could not marry before one year while the boy is moved to another part of the colony. Yet they are not prevented from meeting each other, and under such a slack system it often happens that the girl again becomes a mother before the year has passed.

Such a system tends to breed immorality instead of discouraging it. The government should take charge of the property and divide it pro-rata between those who have produced the wealth. At least each worker who has helped to produce that wealth should be paid a reasonable wage for every day's work that he performed while a member of the colony. All were required to sign a release before they were allowed to leave. The leaders of the colony today own land and factories worth several millions of dollars, all made through a system of slavery on American soil. Free the slaves and return them the fruits of their labors.

* * * * * *

We might add to the above from the Rock Island News, *...that the Amana colony has a great many poor, deluded, ignorant Germans who come along, or who are imported. These men are hired at a wage in money and a few gallons of wine per month. The men are kept by the colony folks at these starvation wages as long as the men are able to work. But as excesses of wine creep into their physical systems and the men are incapacitated for work, they are sent over to the Iowa County Home. Fully seventy-five percent of the county charges in the county home have come there after having given the Amana Society all their active lives. If you question this statement, ask the steward of the County Home or investigate the records for yourself. Another thing, the percentage of insanity is fifty percent higher in Amana township than it is in any other township in the county. It is thought that this high rate of insanity is caused from degeneracy attendant upon intermarriage, and by over-indulgence in wine, liquors, and other excesses. And in the face of these facts there is occasionally a magazine writer who will spread the salve and call the Amanaites [sic.] "a wonderful people."* —Ed. Sentinel

Amana Society Response

From the archives, Amana Heritage Society, printed in 1918.

At various times during the period of the war, malicious and libelous attacks, with charges of disloyalty, were made on our society. These attacks were principally engendered by business jealousy and race prejudice, the ancestors of most of the present members having been German.

To let the truth be known, we submit the following facts:

The society purchased $133,000 of Liberty Bonds.

The members of the society purchased $22,000 of War Savings Stamps.

The society contributed $3,825 to the Red Cross.

The society contributed $4,350 to the Army YMCA and other war welfare work.

The society donated $750 to Armenian Relief.

A separate branch of the Red Cross is maintained within the society with a membership of over 1,000.

The school children of the society are 100 percent Junior Red Cross.

More than 300 garments for soldiers were knit by the women of the society.

5,000 pounds of Belgian relief clothing were donated by members of the society.

250 pounds of shells were gathered by the children of the society.

Twenty-eight members of the society served in the Army.

Two of the four active physicians of the society served in the army as commissioned officers and the other two were members of the Volunteer Medical Service Corps.

All food regulations were scrupulously observed within the society.

The manufacturing facilities of the society were placed at the disposal of the government.

Do these facts indicate disloyalty, or a sincere effort to assist our government?

Soldiers Visit the Amana Colonies

**Great Day's Outing for the Commercial Club
and Training Detachment**

Iowa City Citizen, August 7, 1918

About 160 soldier mechanics of the university training detachment had the time of their lives in a visit to the Amana Colonies yesterday. The forty members of the Iowa City Commercial Club who took their cars and transported the soldiers there also had a great day. And from the expressions of the people of Amana, who were the wholehearted hosts of the occasion, the colony people likewise received great pleasure from the occasion.

(After a traditional Amana dinner, boxing exhibitions by the soldiers, war songs by the soldiers' glee club and patriotic speeches, the visitors went to the woolen mills to get a firsthand look at the making of U.S. army blankets.)

The Amana woolen mills have been famous throughout the country for more than a generation for the flannels and blankets produced. They have the most up-to-date machinery and the products sell rapidly to the largest stores in the country. The Marshall Field company of Chicago has taken some of their goods but their biggest single customer is Macy's department store in New York City, which buys as many as 1,500 pairs of blankets at an order. Just now the mills are running on government contracts only and turning out all-wool khaki colored blankets, the appearance and texture of which delighted the soldiers. To illustrate how the reputation of the Amana goods is gained, the superintendent showed a government sample which is the standard to which they are working and the blankets just off the loom were of a better texture than the sample required. In other words, the Amana Society is giving more under their contract than they are required to do.

The colonists are giving evidence of their loyalty to the United States government and are strong in their protests against the misrepresentations they say have been made about them merely because they are a German community. Most of them were born in the community, but they come from German parentage and have retained the German

103

language and many of the German customs. Theirs is the most remarkable experiment in community living in the United States and possibly in the world. These 1,600 people have all their goods in common and groups of five to seven families, perhaps thirty persons, have their common kitchen and dining room in which the help problem is solved by the women who are assigned to this part of the work. Each family has its own separate house with living rooms and bedrooms. The members have little need of money and receive only a small amount, but all their wants are supplied from the community fields and the community stores without exchange of money.

The Amana community furnished no volunteers to the Civil War, but they have thirty-one of their boys who have gone into training and are assigned to the non-combatant branch of the service because of their religious scruples against war. The leaders of the community, however, say that they recognize the greatness of the present war and are thoroughly loyal to the government. The American flag was seen everywhere in the colonies yesterday. The Liberty loan honor flag from the federal reserve headquarters was flying just below the Stars and Stripes, on the flag pole at Old Amana. The Red Cross work is thoroughly organized in the colonies and the young people talk with pride of the boys who have gone into the army and mentioned some, not living in the community recently, who voluntarily enlisted in the army. Service flags are seen in some of the homes. Judge Wade's intensely patriotic speech was received with great interest and hearty applause on the part of the colony people. One of the older men, who said he was neither an elder nor trustee, but merely one of the workers, stated he never heard a speech like that. He believed in it, he said, and although he was born in Alsace, his heart was with America. He said, also, that whatever sentiment might be found in the colonies among individuals, the ruling elders and trustees were loyal, teaching the people right things and doing all they could to help the government. This was a fine tribute to the spirit of the governing council of the colonies.

The Amana people are law-abiding. Formerly they had their own breweries, German fashion, but discontinued them as soon as Iowa law prohibited the manufacture of beer. Last year they destroyed many thousand gallons of wine after the last prohibitory enactment made the manufacture of it illegal.

An interesting phase of their loyalty is that they are doing their best to obey Governor Harding's language proclamation. It would be natural that a community attempting to keep itself separated form the rest of the world should maintain the native language of its people. Many of the older colonists do not understand English. But now they have changed the instruction in their schools so that it is in English, and, to my surprise, they informed me that they have modified their religious service in German, something which is a real deprivation to the older people who understand no other language. They want to keep themselves above suspicion. Newspapers and magazines are taken very largely, and consigning their peculiar customs one gains the impressions that the Amana people are striving to do their full duty toward their government they appreciate.

About a dozen men from the Amana Colonies served in non-combat roles in World War I. Pictured in uniform is Dr. Christion Herrmann with his niece, Louise Miller. This self-portrait by Dr. Herrmann, a noted amateur photographer, is from the collection of his daughter, Ruth Schmieder.

The Amanas
Iowa's Communist Success

Chariton Iowa Leader, May 22, 1923
By J.B. Scannell

Uncontrollable turmoil in the world today brings to the minds of Iowans thoughts of a little group of peaceful villages nestling among the gentle hills and fertile valleys of eastern Iowa County. Students in government turn here with quickened interest and understanding to the largest communistic organization outside of Russia, in fact, the only really successful community of its kind in the world, the Amana Community of Iowa. What success is the Amanas having?

From the train or the tourist auto whirling through on the Red Ball route, all of the houses and all of the people seem alike as though cut, years ago, from some grotesque pattern by an Arabian magician. Indeed, a picture of age and unchangeability is the first impression gained by the casual observer or the superficial sociologist. It is easy enough to conjure up visions of Hendrick Hudson's mariners from the "Half Moon" sleeping with Rip Van Winkle in the somnolent Catskills, so unusual and unnatural seem the surroundings.

The colonies have built up a good retail business with neighbors and a wholesale business all over the country, so that Amana woolens and calicos are known from coast to coast for quality and dependability. Amana farm products and grain mills are the envy of others.

Indeed, there would be no questioning their stability, now or at any time, were it not that every experiment of a similar nature has failed or is now on the verge of failure. The Icarian Community, which once took over the site of the Mormon settlement at Nauvoo, Ill., no longer exists; the Shakers, well known in the East, have perished through the seeds of their own doctrines; the Oneida Community of New York has dwindled in faith and numbers to the status of a mere commercial corporation. The House of David, of Detroit, a recent experiment, is in the toils of the law, and the same tale of degeneration and disintegration may be traced through the entire history of other communist sects.

"But Amana is proving a notable exception to the general rule," says Bertha M. Shambaugh, who has spent many weeks visiting in the colonies. "I believe they are more successful because they have made religion the main reason for their segregation. They have kept pure the faith of their founders and have avoided the false conception of family life which has wrecked so many promising communities."

....

Recently a Sunday newspaper printed a sensational feature story which intimated that the Amanas are doomed, being much weakened by the loss of about 300 younger members. This article is emphatically denied by the elders and is just as emphatically disputed by Mrs. Shambaugh, who knows more about the intimate life of the community than any other outsider.

It is true, according to Mrs. Shambaugh, and confirmed by the elders, that the total membership is less than it was thirty years ago, at about the time Mrs. Shambaugh's book, the only authorized version of the Amana life, was published. But this shrinkage is not due to the loss of young people. At that time there were well over 200 celibate members, whose ideas of marriage were similar to the theory held and practiced by the Shakers. These members were still reflecting the influence of Shaker association in the east. Naturally they left no offspring. These members with their unnatural philosophy are gone.

Of course, it is well known that members do leave the colony. There is no law compelling them to stay. Almost invariably they return after a tussle with unnatural competition outside, chastened in spirit and still more convinced of the reliability of their own manner of living. Also, the community frequently receives voluntary recruits from the outside. Such people are welcome if it is certain that their faith and intentions meet the sect requirements. It becomes apparent that the balance has been pretty well-held, in the main, that the community is holding its own. This is a most remarkable achievement, when one considers the many radical changes which have taken place in the world during the past century.

Strictly speaking, the Amanas are not a study in sociology, but in theology. The community does not practice communism for the mere economic benefits but for the larger reason that the system seems to offer the best method of leaving them free to practice their religious beliefs in peace.

One acquainted with the people can hardly doubt their ability to hold the community together during the succeeding centuries, even though there is a tendency to doubt the appearance in the near future of another member with the "True Inspiration." There has been none since Barbara Heinemann, and she seemed, after the inspired manhood of Christian Metz, to possess many ideas not in keeping with strict spirituality.

"But all that is in the hands of God," say these pious members, some of whom are direct descendants of Christian Metz and may be themselves the immediate precursors of another great leader who is destined soon to lead the people to renewed faith and still greater achievement. But sham is so readily detected by them that it will take a real prophet to win support.

The writer noticed that there has been a marked change in general atmosphere about the colonies during the last ten years. This change is purely external, the elders say. Changes are partly due to a gradual Americanization process, not at all discouraged by the wisest leaders. Most of the members born in Germany or who came here from New York are now gone, although age creeps up slowly in the peaceful village life. Johanna Geiger and one other woman lived to over a hundred. One old man is now about ninety-two.

Store clothes are being substituted for homemade goods and many of the younger girls are copying styles seen outside, bringing back modern ideas of dress and decoration after visits to outside friends. But there is still no tendency to break away from the old ideals of simplicity that have made life long and pleasant, and increased the average length of life.

One member, a close student of conditions within as well as outside the colonies, is of the opinion that their communal life would be just as successful on a larger scale, even as large as Iowa, if the same faith could be maintained. He admitted, however, that difficulties of holding faith would increase if the community became too large to give the personal touch and intimate contact so largely responsible for Amana's success.

Such are the Amanas of today—changing, yet unchangeable; friendly, yet unyielding; jealous of their doctrines but tolerant of others' beliefs....

COMMUNITY CHANGE

Excerpts from

Fire Greatest Loss of Amana in Eighty Years

Ruins...Unfamiliar Scene...in Picturesque Setting
"Second Blow in Week"

Marengo Republican, August 15, 1923
By Jim Farquhar

As I stand tonight in the gathering twilight amid the charred ruins of what this morning was the industrial center of the greatest and only successful communistic settlement out of forty-nine experiments attempted in the United States, my thoughts revert to memories of my childhood...amid the quaint mills now but haunting spectres of their former picturesque grandeur.

Peter Zimmerman, for long years the benevolent head and guiding genius of the colossal industry famed for the excellence of its products for over one-half a century from coast to coast, stands nearby with heavy heart and gives voice to the thought, "these ruins are all that remain to tell the story of the work of years of toil," but with the Christian philosophy which has been the marvel of the wondering world...and no thought of vengeance against the unknown miscreant who with the insane mania of incendiarism fired the flour mill at 11:30 o'clock yesterday morning and started the half million dollar blaze.

"The Amana Colony has suffered two grevious blows in the past two days," said August Wendler of High Amana. "One was the terrible fire we just experienced, the other was the death of President

109

Harding, the services on whose behalf on Friday were attended by every colonist and the grief over which would have been no more sincere had we lost the president of our own Society."

....

There is something incongruous about such a scene of havoc and pathos amidst so picturesque a setting. On one side of the romantic little bridge crossing the canal, all is in ruins. On the other side there reclines against the railing a sweet-faced colony child....

Photograph of fire from the Leonard Graf collection, Museum of Amana History.

Excerpts from

Fire Destroys Amana Mills

Ten Buildings Wiped Out In Saturday Afternoon Blaze Despite Firefighters' Efforts

Marengo Republican, August 15, 1923

Amid the peaceful vine-clad and flower bedecked homes of Amana, the cry of fire resounded just as they were enjoying their noonday meal Saturday. Within three hours an inferno of flames had destroyed the colony's two great industries, the flouring mills and the woolen mills. Ten great buildings burned with a fury before which hundreds of firefighters were powerless and the loss is conservatively estimated at $250,000. It may run much higher, some estimates place it at half a million.

The buildings destroyed were the big grain elevator, the flouring mill, with several corn cribs and an office building on one side of the mill race and connected by the power house, which was also destroyed; the wool washing building, a great wool finishing building and the dye house. East of these, in a line on the east side, were three buildings used for the storage of wool. One of these was of brick and the walls are left standing. The other two of frame were totally destroyed. On the north side of the fire area was a long brick building used for the bleaching of blankets and for carpet weaving. This was only partially destroyed....The power plant, including all the machinery,...and the office building are a total loss together with the corn crib and other small structures.

Carried Own Insurance

The Society carried its own insurance....It is not at all dismayed by the loss. The structures will be rebuilt almost immediately, on a larger and better plan. They will be in separate groups hereafter so that the dangerous flour mill with dust explosions and other perils will not be connected to the woolen mills by a common power house as it had been.

Work Will Go On

The work of the Society will not be greatly hampered. The mill at

111

Middle Amana will be run on double shift. New machinery will be ordered at once from the east....In the meantime buildings will be put up ready for its reception. The great weaving building of the woolen mills was not harmed and the finishing building still has its walls standing.

The Society is fortunate also in having its big print mill, which has been idle since the war made it impossible to get German dyestuffs. This machinery and the power plant will now be put to good service. It came into immediate use yesterday afternoon when the fire destroyed the other power plant which had been furnishing the colony's water pressure. The other engine was started and the colony suffered practically no inconvenience.

But that was partly because of the calm and resigned way in which members of the Society are in the habit of taking whatever misfortune may come and doing their best to turn misfortune into a blessing.

....

Alarm at 11:30

At 11:30 a young man named Fred Schmeider saw a puff of smoke and a flash of flames coming from one of the windows of the first floor of the flour mill. Rushing to the home of P.C. Geiger, who was in charge of the mills, he shouted: "The mills are on fire!" Geiger was taking a little noon nap. He sprang to the fire bell and gave the alarm.

At Work in Seven Minutes

Within seven minutes the big hand fire engine, with fifteen men on each side, was sending a four-inch stream of water upon the flames. But by this time there was an inferno of flames in the basement of the mills, and every few minutes a dust explosion would send a long gush of flames shooting towards the firemen. They were compelled to fall back and see the flames leap up and destroy the entire structure, 100 feet wide and three stories high....

Meanwhile calls had been sent for help to the other colonies and they all responded as fast as possible....A call was put in for Marengo and the firefighters from that place, under Fire Chief William Brauch, responded and did valiant service.

The Flames Spread

The flour mill was built in a triangle shape and in the apex of the angle, the flames roared. They soon communicated with the elevator, a frame structure 75 feet high containing 4,000 bushels of wheat, 5,000 of ear corn, 500 of shelled corn, 2,000 bushels of rye and a carload of oats. Nothing that the firemen could do could stop the rush of the flames.

Other Help Arrives

Help came from Iowa City speedily....They came from Victor, from Williamsburg and from Oxford....they worked furiously helping the colonists fight the flames.

....

Cedar Rapids Could Not Help

It was hoped that Cedar Rapids with her effective fire fighting apparatus would be able to rush to the scene to help subdue the conflagration. But the roads were thought to be too rough to permit such a long trip overland. An effort was made to load one of the engines upon a flat car and a start was made, but by this time, it was learned that the fire was under control.

....

Two Men Injured

Two men were overcome by the smoke and had to be carried away to receive medical attention. They were Edward Piper and Joseph Novak. Dr. Noe cared for them and in a comparatively short time, they were out of danger. Several others received minor bruises and cuts.

Was It Incendiary?

The question remains; what caused the fire? Was it a dust explosion in the flour mill? That seems hardly possible since only a small portion of the mill machinery was running....Was it incendiary? There are many who believe that it was, including County Attorney J.P. Gaffney of Williamsburg, who says there have been several fires of undoubted incendiary origin in the southern part of the county.

One Man Arrested

Color was given to the rumor of incendiarism when Dan Graham was arrested on suspicion and taken by Constable John Kippenam before Secretary Moerschell, who is also a justice of the peace.

Complaint was made against this man by a Negro who goes by the name of John Miller....He declared that he had seen Graham running away from the burning building just as the fire was discovered. But there were no other witnesses to corroborate his story, and Graham was able to establish a fairly good alibi. He had been working in the vicinity and ate his dinner at the colony at 11:30.

The negro claimed that he had known Graham in the penitentiary at Joliet and that Graham had admitted to him that he was a "fire bug." But this story could not be substantiated. Graham was white and shaking; he seemed almost like an insane man, but he nevertheless was able to produce a few facts which seemed to establish his innocence, and he was accordingly released.

Mr. Moerschell Not Revengeful

Secretary Moerschell took this aspect of the matter with great calmness and desires to be just and merciful to the accused men. He said that so far there was not a shred of real evidence against them, and that punishing them would not give the society back its buildings and its machinery and materials.

*Photograph by F.W. Miller, Louise M. Du Val collection,
Museum of Amana History.*

Little Saved From Amana Mill Ruins

Cedar Rapids Gazette, August 1923

Work among the ruins of the elevator, the flouring mill, the power plant and the rest of the ten fire swept buildings at Amana shows that there will be little, if any, salvage....

It is feared that all the boilers and engines are a total loss. As the items in the long list of losses are checked up, the total grows large and disheartening.

Yet the leaders of the colony will not be discouraged. Work of cleaning out the burned buildings and making use of all that can be salvaged is going forward rapidly.

. . . .

Tens of Thousands of Automobiles There

Tens of thousands of automobiles visited the scene of the disaster Sunday. They began arriving early in the morning and continued until late in the evening....They came from all the towns in a radius of fifty miles and many from a much longer distance....

Hard Day's Work for Traffic Officers

It was the hardest day's work the colonists have had—and they grieved that it should come on a Sunday. The rush of visitors into the ruins of the buildings was so great that it was necessary to stretch ropes to keep them out, lest harm befall them.

Dozens of strong men had to be stationed as traffic officers and watchmen. It was difficult to keep the automobiles moving. And it was practically impossible for the automobiles to move in more than one direction. Finally the congestion became so great that the autos had to pass the scene of the fire over the bridge of the mill race and continue to Homestead, west to South Amana, north to West Amana and thence to their destinations on this side of the Iowa River.

History of Amana Colony

Marengo Pioneer, October 1924

There is much in the life of the people of Amana that seems plain and monotonous to the outside world. Yet one is compelled to acknowledge that in many respects theirs is a more rational and ideal life than that which is found in the average country village. It is more genuine and uniform. There is less extravagance; no living beyond one's means; no keeping up of "appearances," and fewer attempts to pass for more than one is worth.

It is apparent that that isolation from the "world" for which the Amana Society has so earnestly striven and which it has so jealously guarded for six generations becomes less and less easy to preserve. The railroad and airplane, the telephone and telegraph, the newspaper and magazine, the endless procession of automobiles, and the great World War have at last brought the community and the "world" so close together that marked changes are taking place in the customs of the people and in their attitude toward life.

Amana's simple doctrine of "Brothers all as God's children" is maintained even in death. In the cemetery there are no family lots, no monuments. The departed members of each village are buried side by side in the order of their death in rows of military precision, regardless of birth, family or spiritual rank. The graves are marked by a low stone or white painted head-board.

Today the community is a living history of all of the work and character and ideals that have been associated with it in the past, and when one looks into the faces of the splendid young men and women to whom it has been handed on as a precious inheritance, when the chant of the "primer class" is heard as it floats out of the vine-covered school window, it is known that in spite of external modifications and adjustments, in spite of the occasional "emblem of vanity" and "worldly amusement," in spite of the inevitable "black sheep" in the fold, much of the beautiful spirit of "the old defenders of the faith" still pervades the community....

Stores in Colony Carry Complete Stocks of Goods

One of Stores Has Complete Line of Furniture and Implements—All Handle Mill Products

Marengo Pioneer, October 1924

Practically nothing usually found in general stores throughout the state is missing in the seven big stores conducted in as many of the towns of the Amana Society, and not only do the Amana people trade there, but people from the surrounding farms.

The stocks in all instances are large, the merchandise is of good quality and everything is sold on a small margin of profit. Among the many lines carried, will be found many of the standard grocery brands, dry goods, notions, ready-to-wear, work clothing, hats, caps, crockery and queensware, cigars, tobaccos, candies, fruits, vegetables—everything the most exacting might call for.

One of the stores carries an extensive line of furniture and agricultural implements, and makes a specialty of fruits grown on land belong to the society, and people drive there from great distances to purchase these by the bushel.

In all of the stores, the highest market prices are paid farmers for their produce, and the patronage enjoyed by them is extensive.

Hog Remedies Made by Amana Society Famous Throughout Wide Area...

Marengo Pioneer, October 1924

...have been on the market for fifteen years and the plant has capacity of turning out twenty-thousand pounds daily and also makes and sells self-feeders which are in great demand.

Hog remedies, manufactured by the Amana Society, have been famous in this section of Iowa for more than 15 years, and today the demand for those products, which are manufactured under the jurisdiction of F.W. Miller, is enormous.

Fifteen years ago the society started the manufacture, by hand power, of Amana hog powder, Amana worm powder and worm capsules. Today there is a modern plant, operated by a gasoline engine, at the rear of the Amana drugstore, and it has a capacity of about 20,000 pounds a day.

In this plant is a sifter, manufactured by members of the society, and a modern mixer, all conveniently arranged so as to save the hard part of the labor. There is also a warehouse for raw materials and for the finished product.

Amana hog remedies are sold extensively within a radius of 35 miles of the colonies, and the customers are looked after personally by attachés of the plant. The use of Amana hog remedies doubled between 1921 and 1923 and is steadily increasing, as the preparations are doing just exactly what is claimed of them.

The first batch of Amana hog powder was made as an experiment, and there were but 300 pounds of it, but so successful did it prove that the output jumped into the thousands of pounds.

Amana hog remedies are sold direct to the user, thus eliminating the agent's profit. They are recommended for all hogs, big and little, at all times of the year, and help to keep them healthy—stimulating the appetite, aiding digestion and assimilation, and regulating the bowels.

The Iowa Amana Society
This Is the One Successful Communistic Settlement in State

Chariton Leader July 31, 1928 (reprinted from *Wallaces' Farmer*)

This summer, for the first time in fourteen years, I called on George Heinemann, the president of the Amana Society. He was seventy years old in 1914, but today he seems no older.

I found it interesting to listen to a conversation between Harvey Ingham, the dean of Iowa editors, and this patriarch of the Amana community. The simple religious faith of the old man interested Mr. Ingham greatly....a faith which enabled the pioneers to conquer the wilderness, the faith which enabled his own father to hold out under difficult circumstances, the faith which has almost disappeared in this scientific age. Mr. Heinemann's face is peaceful, but there is a spiritual gleam to his eye and a quickness to his mind...

In these rapidly changing times, even the Amana people have changed some. There are still no moving picture houses in any of the seven Amana villages, but there are several automobiles....owned by the society and not by individual members, because it is hard for an individual member to get together enough money to buy an auto. The members receive from the society, in addition to their board and room, less than $100 a year....they don't need to worry about saving up money for their old age or for sickness because they know that the society will take care of them...Young women with children are happier...they are relieved from their kitchen duties and household cares and can center their attention almost exclusively on their children.

The Amana people are leading a simple, healthy kind of life...Their standard of living, however, is lower than that of the average Iowa farmer....Should the Iowa farmer stop his fight for a fair share in the national income? Should he stop trying to live like the people in town? Should he make less use of automobiles and radios and things of that sort? If the farmers of the United States are willing to set themselves off...different from the people in town, living in a simpler way, they can probably be quite happy.

Communistic Pillar of the Amanas Totters Before Modernism

Ideals, Customs Waver Before Advances Made by the Outside World — Generations of Self-denial and Brotherly Love Have Not Destroyed Embers of Enterprise and Individualism — Religious Fervor Weakening — A Stock Corporation Favored to Supplant Communism

Cedar Rapids Gazette, June 21, 1931
By Adeline Taylor

Ideals have betrayed the Amanas. Brotherly love and faithful devotion flourished for ninety years in America's only successful communistic colony. To cultivate such Utopian standards one must wall out worldly distractions. They did, these True Inspirationists. They sought isolation on the prairie frontier of the Midwest when they came to Iowa in 1855. And they hung a sign on their front door which read, "Please pass by and leave us alone." No welcome mat could have held more attraction. The world from which they fled swarmed to them to find out "what there is so private going on here."

Autos, airplanes, highways, telephones, radios have assailed those secluded walls until each stronghold has given way. And against the tripled speed of modern America, the tranquillity of Amana stood out still more quaintly calm by comparison.

Visitors Hold Up Mirror for Colonists

Curiosity seekers, writers, students, tourists passed through, leaving seeds of discontent and worldliness behind them. They held up mirrors of these quaint people and left them wondering, "Why should we be so different from the rest of the world?" And they painted such glorious pictures of the society from which they came that many from the Amana Society have stepped forth to taste its sweets.

The record book of the president of the Amanas, George Heinemann, lists 1,378 residents today. An Amana feature story in this paper five years ago quotes the population at 1,800.

It was a strange world that the curiosity seeker found. He saw many things to exclaim over—no hospitals or doctor bills, no jails or courts or lawyers, no banks, no poverty or wealth, no penniless old age, no paint, no wallpaper—only trees that bore fruit—no family dinner tables, no divorces or elopements, no automobiles, no theaters and entertainments, no wages, no keeping up appearances.

Foundation of the Society Is Religion

Amana is called a communism, but that is only one of its pillars. The foundation of the society rests on religion. The name Amana itself is a biblical term which means to believe faithfully.

The communistic pillar is swaying today because the religious foundation is slipping. Five generations of self-denial and brotherly love, ninety years of believing faithfully have not destroyed the human sparks of jealousy and suspicion nor the embers of enterprise and of a madly rushing and money-seeking world to fan them into flame. All the money from farm and factory goes into a common fund and a maintenance sum is allowed each individual ranging from $25 to $50 or more a year. Variations lately have caused jealousy and discontent.

No Cash Paid the Members for Labor

No cash is paid the society members for their labors. Their services go into credit on the books against which purchases are charged, and no check is kept nor regular reckoning made. There are rumors of private bank accounts and suspicions of land owned outside the colony.

Time was at Amana when chemists' prescriptions were stolen and copied, calico designers' ideas duplicated, new mill devices lifted and patented, without disturbing the tranquillity of the village. It is different now. The world has stepped in to show the glamorous future of such enterprises for themselves.

Youth has always extended its vitality, but the religious fervor of Amana once kept that vigor in the right channel. That fervor is dying out. Church ostracism has become a privilege instead of a punishment. The hours of worship grow shorter and the attendance declines. The world has brought in too many diversions on a Saturday night to make church on a Sunday morning appear inviting. The young people smile knowingly and perhaps a little skeptically at the idea of the older members that the curse of God will descend on them if they give up communism and the habits of their founders. They want ways to exploit their rights—cars to take them places, amusements to entertain them when they get there, private goals to work toward.

The ideal of remaining faithful, the religious foundation of true believing, is moving away and another must be found, it seems, if Amana is to continue its existence.

Business Corporation May Be the Substitute

It does not seem strange then, does it, that the world which stormed the walls of this secluded valley should now attempt to rear its flag starred with dollar signs and striped with literal gains over the citadel. The most popular plan for reorganization is that of substituting a business corporation for a religious communism. The visions in this plan are countless as you survey the 26,000 acres of the richest bottomland and the most fertile upland in Iowa.

The successful exploitation of one industry stands as a testimonial to the outcome of these dreams—Amana blankets. No other spot in the world produces better woolens, blankets, dress goods and flannels than Amana. These products are sold in every state in the Union. The Amana woolen mills, the first to be erected in Iowa, have been in active operation for fifty years. They use more than a half-million pounds of wool annually. Their 3,000 sheep can't furnish it all—they must buy from outside markets, principally Chicago.

And there are just as many possibilities in the commercialization of the rest of Amana products. Sixteen thousand of their fertile acres—now valued when the market is down to rock bottom at $75 an acre—are under the plow. About twelve tractors are owned; much of the rest of the work is done by hand. Every department of agriculture is "functionated." In each branch, the lieutenant looks to the boss who is responsible to the board of trustees for proper execution. Their agricultural products—rye, barley, oats.

Other Products Are in Great Demand

There are other industries flourishing on a small scale in Amana which attract the neighboring citizens to markets where only the best is made. Amana winter cured hams—the demand is never satisfied. Amana bread and Amana cheese remain in a category by themselves. Imagine the canning possibilities in a village where the strawberries grow as big as plums; cauliflowers are ten inches across...

Amana, Iowa's Old Communal Settlement, Is Feeling the Stir of a "Revolt" of its Youth

Kansas City Star, June 28, 1931
By A.B. MacDonald

Young women of the strange colony, established 75 years ago, already have "gone modern" as regards to bobbed hair and short skirts, and there is a growing sentiment against the ban on electric lights, radios, games, music and privately owned motor cars. The sect's property in Iowa, all owned in common, is worth $3 million. All dine in community houses where women take turns in cooking and serving food.

Coming to the top of a hill on the highway of concrete that stretches eastward from Des Moines, there appears before us a long, level valley of the Iowa River, with the seven villages of the Amana Society sitting amid the fields of corn and wheat and broad pastures where herds of cattle grazed.

"That's the place we have come to see," I said to my son, who was driving the car.

"Those shabby-gray towns? Are they too poor to paint their houses? They ought to name it Hardscrabble," he said.

"Poor! That is one of the richest communities in this country," I replied. "They own 26,000 acres of the richest farming land in all the world."

"Then why don't they spread a little paint?"

"It's contrary to their religious convictions to paint their houses," I explained. "They hold that paint smeared on houses is worldly, a luxury, and a showing of vanity and pride. This is a religious society that believes in living apart from the world and all its bumps and trivialities."

It had been twenty years since I had visited Amana. At that time I had asked one of the elders,…"Wouldn't it be economy to paint these old frame houses; they would last longer and look better?"

"They might," he replied. "But paint is a sinful waste and belongs to the pomps and vanities of the world. We have figured it out that it will cost about as much to keep a house painted for 50 or 100 years as it would to build a new one after it has fallen into decay."

But today when I talked with one of the younger men of Amana, a leader in the revolt against what he called "religious old-fogyism," he said:

"It's a rotten policy not to paint our houses. The state has built a cross-state highway of concrete right through the community and thousands of cars pass daily. They see our villages, all unpainted, and a barren gray from the weather, and they naturally conclude, just as your son did, that we are too poverty-stricken to paint them. They turn up their noses at us and drive straight through. An unpainted town is a bad advertisement. We want a new deal so we can paint our houses white, as other towns are painted."

Twenty years ago, and even up to five years ago, the women of Amana wore the same style of dress their ancestors wore in Germany 200 years ago. All made their own clothing. It was of plain calicoes in gray or blue or brown. All wore aprons and shoulder shawls of black, with a small black cap, or sunbonnet in summer, and a heavy black hood in winter. The hair of the young women and girls was worn in long braids down their backs.

But there has been a rebellion of the young people. I saw groups of girls today with bobbed hair and short skirts. And one of them said to me:

"We are sick and tired of this old-fogyism that masquerades as religion. It isn't religion, it's darned foolishness. When bobbed hair and short skirts came in, many of us girls in Amana wanted to follow the fashions and dress like all the other young women of the towns around us. But no. We are told that short skirts and short hair were sinful. The women of our society had never changed their style of dress for 200 years. The waist was short and skirt long and full.

"The old fogies threatened to expel us if we broke away from those hateful styles, but there were too many of us. Look around and you see that nearly all the young women and the girls wear short skirts and bobbed hair. We are free at last and we are going to stay free and be like other folks. They can't tell us younger women that a woman's

124

morality and Christianity depend on the way she wears her hair. We can go bare-legged and wear bathing suits and still be Christians. It's not in the way you dress, it's what's in your heart that decides whether you are a Christian or not."

The young people in Amana have not achieved motor cars yet, for their elders declare that cars, too, are "worldly," and therefore sinful, but the young men and women are in revolt and will get them and the other things that go with life in modern American towns, for the Amana Society is menaced by mutiny and disorganization.

Amana is the richest and one of the oldest communist colonies in America. Its 1,390 members own in common three million dollars worth of property, including 26,000 acres of fertile land and seven villages, with factories, mills, stores, warehouses, barns, farming machinery and the like. And there is not a dollar of debt against any of it.

For seventy-five years the Amana Society has gone along, a colony of religious communists, in the heart of the best farming district in Iowa, holding themselves aloof from the world and its levities, having peculiar customs and religious beliefs, preserving the habits of two centuries ago, a bit of old German in the midst of new America.

People have gone from all parts of the world to see and study Amana. Thousands of newspaper and magazine articles and pamphlets have been written about this communistic settlement. For more than three-quarters of a century, it has been pointed out as proof that communism is a practical and workable system. Other experiments in communism have failed. Oneida, Brook Farm, New Harmony, Icaria, Zoar and many others have come and gone their way, but this Iowa colony has lived on, faithful to its name, "Amana," a Bible term meaning "remain true."

Now there is insubordination and rebellion within its ranks and it faces dissolution. The majority of the young people do not want to be the Mystics and Pietists their forefathers were. They do not subscribe to the Amanist doctrine that the world is simply a corridor to heaven in which man abides for a little while solely that he may have time and opportunity to work out his future salvation. They believe they can have religion and yet have a good time in this world. They do not want to be peculiar in dress and manners and ways of living.

They want to give up the German tongue and be an American community. They are tired of being pointed at as "odd people."

There is another class in Amana made up of men of middle-age who have slowly come to realize that communism, without a deeply-rooted religious zeal to uphold it, is a failure. They see that the old mysticism and religious fervor that held the colony together is fast dying out and giving place to broader views, and without that religious ideal the community cannot be held together much longer. They hold it would be better to reorganize and have a new deal, voluntarily, now, than to have it come by a complete upheaval and disruption later on.

Still another class, composed of the elderly men and women, opposes any change and wants to go along in the old way. But already the mutiny against their rule is in full swing. Meetings have been held in the different villages and committees have been appointed to work out plans of reorganization that will be submitted to the people.

It has been charged that certain families of the community were given special favors in their matter of homes. I was told by several that one of the serious faults of this communistic way of living was that certain persons of dominating natures gained supremacy and got the best of everything.

Try as they may, the old-fashioned rulers of the community cannot stamp out the love of beautiful things from the souls of the women. Forbidden to paint the houses, they have trellises up on the sides of them, and in summer grapevines clamber and cover the sides of all the houses, making them bowers of green. And each house has its flower garden, and each village is abloom with old-fashioned roses, hollyhocks, dahlias and other flowers.

There is no renting within any of the Amana villages. Each family may furnish and decorate as it sees fit, but any undue extravagance or display would be severely rebuked. A "store carpet" would be looked upon as "worldly" and therefore sinful. The village weavers make rag carpets of beauty. In the village furniture factory all sorts of furniture is made by hand from walnut, ash, cherry and oak that grew in the neighborhood. Even the house hardware is made there, by hand.

In the Amana homes are no electric lights, no music, no radios, no amusements of any kind. They are labeled "worldly" and distract the mind from the contemplation of religion. There are no motor cars, except a few trucks used for business. The lack of these things is source of deep complaint and accounts for the revolt as much as any other cause. A young married woman said to me:

"If electric light is worldly and therefore sinful, the coal oil lamps must be sinful, too, because they are a step in advance of the old tallow candle."

(Teaching of German in the schools and religious classes on Saturdays and after regular schools hours are some of the things sought to be changed by the young mutineers. They want Saturday for play. They want baseball and other games, of which there are none now. The more radical rebels want baseball Sunday afternoons.)

Every night in the year there are religious services and all are supposed to attend. These services are dreary and dull, consisting of the reading of "revelations" by the ancient prophets of the cult and testimonies. The majority of the young people say they want to keep their religion, but they do not want it in such daily overdoses.

Today there is open rebellion against arbitrary assignment of persons to certain work. Many young men and women, given work to do that they do not like, refuse to obey orders. And there is no way to punish them or force them to work. They could be expelled, but expulsion is unpopular and the trustees have trouble enough now. Many men of the community are loafing, refusing to work, or, if they do work, they loaf on the job, but they eat and are clothed and housed just as are those who work and share the burdens of the day.

In the old days this kind of insubordination was very rare and the guilty one was punished by being barred from church services for a period. When I first visited Amana twenty years ago, I found a young man suffering shame and keen mental agony because the trustees were barring him from church for three Sundays as a punishment for playing baseball on Sunday. Today a young man would laugh at a decree of that kind. He would probably say: "We are fed up on religion; anyhow, I prefer to stay away from church for awhile."

And so, there is a demand for a reorganization on some plan that will let a man choose his own work and pay him wages according to his worth as a workman. The movement would remove the old religious Pietists from the management and put in younger men with more modern and progressive ideas who would permit games and motor cars, music and electric lights, and picture shows.

There is no picture show in the community. No show of any kind ever exhibited there. No person owns a motor car. But the young people go to all kinds of shows in the nearby town of Marengo. They are impressed by the difference between Marengo, with its paved streets, its beautiful houses and its theaters and motor cars and modern stores, as compared with their own cheerless village homes and lives. The population of Amana has dwindled from 1,800 to 1,380 in a few years. Many young people go away as soon as they are old enough to shift for themselves.

George Heinemann has been president of the Amana Society for twenty-three years. He is 87 years old. I found him in the big brick house in which he lives with several other members of the society. I asked him for his photograph and he shook his head. He had none.

"Will you please step out into the sunshine; I have a camera and will take a picture of you?" I asked.

"It is forbidden by the Ten Commandments," he said in a mild voice that had a distinct German accent.

"What!" I exclaimed in amazement. "The taking of photographs forbidden? In what commandment?"

"In the very first commandment," he said with a smile, as he repeated it: "Thou shalt not make unto thee any graven image, or any likeness of anything," and he went on to explain:

"When I was a boy I went to Chicago and was induced to have my picture taken, but later, when I realized that God had forbidden it, I burned the picture and prayed for forgiveness. We do not have our pictures taken here; God has forbidden it."

"Have none of your children had their pictures taken?" I asked.

"I have never married," he said. "You want to know why? Because the single state enables a man to be more spiritually-minded. Realizing that God placed me here on earth solely to work out the salvation of my soul, knowing that marriage would hinder me in that seeking after perfection, I decided, when a young man, to take the advice of Paul, who said it was better for a man to remain single. Quite a number of us have never married for that reason."

We were alone in his room. The blinds were drawn and the gloom of the place gave it an air of solemnity. An ancient rag rug covered the floor. The furniture had been made by hand many years ago.

He sat at a stand upon which lay an old German Bible. He was in his shirt sleeves. On his head was an old straw hat. A fringe of gray whiskers hung over his soiled celluloid collar. His trousers, of the cheapest cotton, were much worn and baggy.

I had been told by men, old and young, that he was the most lovable, kindly, benevolent Christian man in the community and that everyone loved him, but a young man added: "He is living in the days of 200 years ago."

In his face was the look of one who had become a Mystic by long years of self-abnegation and silent meditation upon the mysteries of religion. We talked a long time of the movement within the society to reorganize it.

"The same thing is the matter with us that has affected all religious institutions in the outside world," he said. "The young people have lost their fidelity to the old truths of religion. They have become worldly."

He said that automobiles, electric lights, music, games and all that modern "trash" were forbidden, not because of the expense or waste, but because the use of those things would be conforming to the ways of the world and would take the mind off religion.

He went to a bookcase in a corner and smoothed his hand lovingly down its door.

"I made it seventy-five years ago," he said. "It is solid walnut."

He opened the door and showed it filled with very old books, all in German.

"The sacred writings of the prophets of our sect," he said.

Some of the books were printed 200 years ago. They were all filled with the "inspired" utterances of the old prophets, and he said they were as sacred and as authoritative as the Bible.

As we came out into the sunlight, an airplane soared overhead. He took off his hat, the better to look up at it, and he said:

"There it is, the new world with its distractions that is killing religion."

"Will there be a new organization here?" I asked.

"Yes, I think there will be," he answered. "I do not want it. I want to go on as we always have. But the young folks won't have it so."

And then, as he stood in the lawn beside the most beautiful row of black roses I ever saw, he took one of them tenderly into his hand and said:

"Since we began here, there has been some profit every year. We have 26,000 acres of land and we own it and everything on it except the household furniture, and we do not owe a dollar. Since we began eight-six years ago there has never been a year without some profit from our operations. The last two or three years have been the hardest, and that has hastened the young people in their determination to have a change and modernize our methods. But, in those eighty-six years, no person in our community has ever been hungry, or cold, or without shelter and warm clothing. All have been cared for lovingly, with good schooling, good medical care and all legitimate needs supplied, and the salvation of their souls looked after."

He began pulling the petals from the rose and as they fluttered to the ground he continued:

"I am afraid that our people will not be as well cared for and happy in the future as they have been in the past. They will often wish the society was back to the good old times again."

Horsepower 1930s.
Running binders in the field, West Amana.
Photo by Rudolph Kellenberger.

What's What Out on the Acres

Amana Farmer Doesn't Know Yet How Good a Cook His Wife Is; Last Kitchen Meal Next Saturday Crop Manager at Middle Amana

Cedar Rapids Gazette, April 7, 1932

Interview with William Zuber, farm manager at Middle Amana. Born at Middle Amana forty-four years ago.

How will the new system at the Amanas affect your job?

As far as I know, the farms will be handled in the same as they are now. The change may affect me personally. There is no way to tell until it takes place.

How will the change affect the men who work in the field?

Under the new charter each man will be paid according to the amount of work he does. Now all labor is pooled and the returns go to the society.

Will the change be better, in your opinion?

I think it will be possible to operate the farms on more of a business-like basis.

Do you practice rotation?

Yes, we usually follow oats with corn or meadow. We have a three or four year rotation. We raise a great many potatoes, too, and that makes our rotation a little different.

How is your land divided this year?

We have approximately 200 acres in meadow, 200 acres in oats, 200 in corn, 60 acres in potatoes and 100 in wheat. Our potatoes usually go on sod and always on the richest soils.

Do you have much barnyard fertilizer to use?

Yes, a great deal. Ordinarily it is used on the potato ground or on the fields close to the barns.

How do you maintain the fertility in the fields far from the barns?

We aim to seed down regularly.

What do you sow?

Red clover and timothy.

Have you ever used commercial fertilizer?

We have used some on the corn.

What results did you observe?

It seemed to make the corn grow faster in the spring, but we never checked at harvest time to see if we got any bigger yields.

Is your soil fairly rich anyway?

It is good soil but some of it is heavy and sour.

Have you used any lime?

Not much. I think the first thing we need as soon as we can afford it is tile drainage.

Why?

So the fields will be fit to work all over at the same time. We need drainage before we should use lime.

Have you made any acidity tests?

Yes. Practically all of the land shows need of from one-half to two tons of limestone.

Do you have any trouble getting a catch of clover?

It seems of late years that we do. At least it seems as if we don't have as much hay as we used to. We don't let the meadows get too old though and that helps.

Will your farming be more economical and more systematic under the new plan?

It should be. Of course it will take time to get it all worked out. It will come out all right though if the people stick together and have faith that it will.

What kind of an impression does the new business manager, Arthur Barlow, make?

I have seen him and heard him talk just once and I think he made a good impression. He has a big job but he seems to be capable of doing it.

Will the fact that the folk here have been trained to work together make his job and theirs any easier in readjusting themselves to the new conditions?

Yes, that should be a big help. Under the present system, when a person leaves the colonies, he is gone for good. Under the new system, if he is dissatisfied, he can pull out but still can return if he will comply with the provisions of the constitution.

Why did your son sign with the Cedar Rapids Bunnies?

He likes to play ball and we felt that if that's what he wants to do he should do it.

What did he play at Middle Amana?

He pitched and played first base.

When will you have your last meal in the kitchens?

Saturday night we will have our last supper together.

Have you planned a celebration of any kind?

No. I expect the girls will be good to us though and bake an extra cake or two.

Won't it seem peculiar to eat your last meal in the kitchens and change to meals just for your own family?

I seldom have eaten anywhere else but in the kitchens so I don't know what it will be like. In fact I don't know much about home-cooking. I don't even know how good a cook my wife is. You see, she always had someone to cook with her under the kitchen system, but I guess we will get along all right.

Do you favor Hoover's re-election?

I think not. I can't see where he has done much.

What is your attitude toward prohibition?

I never saw any good in prohibition. I think it would be better to permit the sale of beer.

What about wine and hard liquors?

I wouldn't care so much about wine and strong drinks, but I don't consider beer intoxicating or harmful.

Can a man get drunk on beer?

Well, if he takes too much he is not so likely to get drunk, but more sleepy than rough.

For what other reason do you favor a change in the prohibition law?

Sale of beer under government license would provide revenue and reduce taxes, I think. Also I don't believe so many youngsters would be so likely to drink.

Didn't youngsters drink in saloon days?

Maybe but not so much. It was pretty difficult for a boy to get a drink in those days, but now it doesn't seem to make any difference how young he is if he has the money.

Do you favor Brookhart's re-election?

I really don't know. I thought at one time he was a pretty good man, but he doesn't seem to have accomplished much. He makes good speeches but doesn't do much.

How do you cash your crops?

Practically everything that we have produced so far has been consumed by the society.

How many persons do you feed with your livestock and crops?

Middle Amana has between 250 and 300 persons.

Has the present period of economic distress affected the colonies?

It really is better for us under the present system when things are cheap as far as producing livestock is concerned. We buy more grain than we produce to feed the livestock that we butcher.

Then the marketing problem or distribution problem never has affected you?

Not yet. Under the new plan, when it takes effect, we probably will see more and market prices will affect us.

Are your cattle T.B. tested?

Yes. I believe the test law is a good thing.

Do you favor Turner's re-election?

Yes. Turner has been a good man as far as I know. I don't watch state and national politics very much, but I think Turner has been all right.

Do you watch county and township politics?

Well, most of the candidates come to see me.

Will the change in the system mean that many will buy automobiles and radios?

I suppose it will. In fact, several have radios now, and things like automobiles will be bought by individuals as soon as they can afford them.

Will the towns be lighted by electricity?

That is not likely to happen right away. What may result in the future remains to be seen.

Amanas Eat Last Meal as Communists

Cedar Rapids Gazette, April 7, 1932

The Amana colonies Saturday were writing the final chapter of the history of the rise and fall of religious communism in Iowa.

Saturday night the colonists ate their last meal prepared in their community kitchens and served in the dining halls attached to those kitchens.

At this last meal, a visitor was certain he caught a muffled sob from one of the older members.

He was certain he saw glistening eyes give up a tear or two as the colonists laid down their community knife and fork for the last time.

Only a third of the entire colony ate at the community kitchens, since for several years it has been customary for many colonists to take food from the kitchens to their homes to eat.

No meals have been prepared in the homes. Today will bring a great change in the lives of the women, who will, for the first time, prepare food in their own homes.

The women are not entirely unprepared.

"Oh, my, no," they say. "You see, it's always been a rule of the colonies that every girl must learn to cook and sew.

"Each girl always did a certain apprenticeship in the community kitchens."

Several salesmen have visited the colonies during the last week. It didn't do them a lot of good though, because Amana leaders plan to make a gradual change.

Peter Stuck, one of the general committeemen, said that a seven-month "transition period" has been agreed upon.

During this period, which is to last approximately from May 15, 1932, to Jan. 1, 1933, a basic wage of 10 cents per hour will be paid all workers. Families will be given their homes free of rent. Groceries will be supplied to them at cost.

"We think it is unwise to shift too suddenly," Stuck said. "For instance, in an organization such as ours where no wages have been paid, it would be impossible for us to say a gardener should receive 20

135

cents per hour and a doctor $2 per hour.

"For that reason we have agreed to establish the 10 cents per hour basic wage for everything until we can adjust matters."

The change in eating habits, the most radical of the several shifts that are to come in the next four weeks, marked the first outward break in a system that has been religiously adhered to for 90 years.

The actual change-over from a religious communistic organization to a stock cooperative will not come, however, until about June 15.

Stuck said Saturday:

"More than 100 kerosene cook stoves already have been brought into the colonies and set up in the various homes during the last week."

Stuck and John Eichacker, general chairman of the committee on reorganization, said they did not expect gas or sanitary sewers to be put in for some time, possibly as long as two or three years.

Arthur Barlow, former Cedar Rapids business man, last week began his duties as general business manager of the reorganized society.

Barlow will be responsible for all accounts and finances of the new cooperative organization. He will work on a salary and will devote half days to the job.

Numerous colonists Saturday afternoon were preparing the first individual gardens they have ever made. Heretofore, all colonists have worked in the fields with the resulting produce turned into a general community store house.

With the advent of the new plan, however, each colonist has been allotted one-twelfth of one acre for his own individual garden.

Aside from the change in the dining halls, the advent of Barlow, an outsider, and the making of individual gardens, there were no outward appearances of change Saturday.

Life in the colonies was continuing as heretofore.

"Well, we're going to do it," was the sentiment. "We voted for it."

THE GREAT CHANGE AND CORPORATE LIFE

**Amana Women Turn Cooking Arts to Feeding
Five Instead of Fifty Mouths**

As Kitchens Close

Cedar Rapids Republican, April 10, 1932

Amana colonists ate their last supper cooked in community kitchens Saturday night. For ninety-one years in Iowa, and for two centuries before in Germany, it had been the custom for the Amanans to gather three times a day in the community dining rooms and eat food cooked in community kitchens. But the colonies are no longer a communism, and the first official act since the beginning of their formative corporation has been the abolishing of these kitchens.

Houses in the colonies are being equipped with kitchens to meet the new demands, and husbands, who have not tasted their wives' cooking in two decades of married life together, will be given an opportunity to judge their culinary arts.

Even those women who have had an active part in the community kitchen work in the past may meet with some difficulties in family cooking. It will not be the same preparing meals for one family of five as it was getting ready to feed ten families of fifty persons in the community kitchen.

Amana Bells Are Silent First Time in 90 Years

Will Ring No More to Send Workers into Fields

Des Moines Tribune, April 11, 1932
By Fred Lazell

The bells which for 90-odd years have summoned Amana colonists to work in the fields and to dine in the community dining halls did not ring Monday morning.

Their silence marked the passing of another of those picturesque traditions and customs which have gone on in this "little bit of Europe in America" year after year despite the increasing inroads of modern life.

For almost a century the old bells atop a steeple in the society's meetinghouses have rung to call the colonists to meals and to send them to their labors in the fields.

But Saturday night the colonists dropped their community kitchens and community dining halls and with them went the historic bell ringing.

Rudolph Kellenberger of West Amana photographed the auction for the contents of the West Amana Meat Market. Community kitchens were sites of other auctions after the Great Change.

Community Colony Goes Capitalistic

U.S.'s Oldest Experiment of this Nature Decides Plan Is a Failure

Times-Union, Rochester, New York, April 25, 1932

After existing for 90 years on a basis of "share and share like" for its members, America's oldest and most successful experiment in "pure" communism has decided that its plan is a failure and is getting ready to change to the ways of capitalism.

Already the vote has been taken and within the near future the 26,000-acre Amana Society colony here, owned by 1,200 members of a German religious sect, will be converted into a cooperative stock company chartered under the laws of Delaware.

Going thoroughly modern, it has hired a Cedar Rapids efficiency expert to direct its affairs.

For nearly a century, the members have pooled their holdings and their labor and shared equally in the returns. Crops have gone to common granaries, the surplus sold and the affairs of the colony administered by a board of trustees who saw to it that each member received food, clothing, shelter and an education. No member drew any money; there was no use for it.

Under the new plan, expected to become effective June 15, individuals will be issued stock in the $2,000,000 company and will receive wages for their work. They also will be allowed to buy or rent their own homes from the corporation.

Communism has failed, the bearded leaders of the Amana colony explain, because the present generation does not have the zeal for common ownership that inspired the founders.

Confident of getting a good living under the "share and share alike" plan, many of the younger members have not worked so hard. As a result, profits have declined and in recent years the colony trustees have been having a hard time trying to make ends meet.

Modernism also enters into the change. The younger generation is tired of living in an atmosphere of 200 years ago, under customs like those that existed when the sect was founded in Germany in 1714. They want automobiles, movies, electric lights, radios and other modern things that the ancient laws of the colony brand as "sinful."

Ambitious ones among the young members also want a chance to get ahead in the world. They are tired of seeing individual industry and initiative stifled under a system that offered no more than the bare necessities of life. Already, the change has begun. The community kitchens in the seven villages of the colony, where the women took turns at cooking the food, have been abandoned. Members now dine in their homes instead of in the community dining halls, where the men sat on one side of the room and the women on the other.

The ancient bells in the meetinghouses, which summoned three generations of colonists to their work in the community fields every day except Sunday, are silent now for the first time in 90 years. The colonists are now planting individual gardens.

It is hard to tell, now, how many changes in social customs will follow the changes in economic methods at the Amana colony, but these doubtless will be equally revolutionary.

For one thing, the young people of the community are said to be very much dissatisfied with the present system of marriages in which all engagements must be approved by a vote of the trustees. After the engagement is approved, the boy and the girl must live in separate villages for one year prior to the ceremony and conduct no courtship of any kind.

The girls, too, object to the ancient rules of the colony which require them to wear the plainest of dresses and wear their hair in braids. Some, bolder than the rest, have already bobbed their hair and modernized their attire, despite the protests of the gray-bearded elders that such things are "sinful...."

The Amana Colony is not only the oldest experiment in "pure" communism in the United States, but has been the most successful. For many years it prospered while similar colonies, promoted by other religious sects, tried it and failed. It continued to prosper until a few years ago, when the third generation began to lose interest in the religious fervor that had inspired their forefathers in founding it....

Ninety Years of Communism for Amanas to be Ended this Evening

Colonies Begin Operating on Corporation Basis Monday
All to Get Same Pay during First Year

Cedar Rapids Gazette, May 1, 1932
By Ray Anderson

Monday morning—a new day.

Destined to be memorable in the history of the Amana Society.

Ninety years of relative communistic security—ended when the sun goes down this Sunday evening.

Tomorrow, the step out into the yet unadventured realm of individual responsibility and opportunity.

What thoughts, what anxieties, what hopes, fears, great expectations at twilight this day in the seven villages along the Iowa River?

For when the sun comes up again, it will light a new world for the colony folk, a world of wages, payrolls and other accouterments of non-communistic endeavor.

A drastic change but not too abrupt as if a hand suddenly were snapped asunder allowing the component parts of the unit to fly apart helter-skelter.

Instead, the beginning, according to wise provision of the trustees and management, of a twelve-month transitional period during which all members of the society will share alike in their collective enterprise.

One year from tomorrow, or thereabouts, it is expected that remuneration may begin according to extent and value of service, but for the present the roughest labor and the best skill will fare the same.

Each adult person for whom there is a job will receive 10 cents an hour this coming year. In addition, each family will have its home and garden rent free, and all may buy the necessities of life at the colony stores at cost plus a minimum handling charge.

Will each person have a job at the start?

Possibly not. The population of the seven towns according to a census taken last Dec. 31 totals 1,587 men, women and children.

All the hired hands will go elsewhere, and they have been numerous under the old regime. But at that there may not be employment for all of the colonists, in which case some may continue a short time under the old system on an allowance until provision can be made....

Application for the corporation charter has not yet been filed with the secretary of state at Des Moines. Attorneys still are working on a few minor changes in the articles of incorporation, but it is expected that these will be completed in a few days and the charter received before the week ends or early next week.

Arthur A. Barlow of Cedar Rapids, who began his duties as general business manger of the entire society on April 1, has his office in the store at Amana. Daily reports on all phases of the combined industrial, agricultural and business enterprise are made to him, and all receipts and disbursements are handled at his office.

Assignments have been made and superintendents and managers appointed insofar as the regular farm, manufacturing, business and professional activities of the society demand. The agricultural managers will have complete charge of all farm operations, including livestock, for each town. Each has been instructed to employ only residents of his town. The managers are: P.C. Geiger, Amana; Richard Schaefer, East Amana; Louis Selzer, Homestead; Theodore Setzer, South Amana; William Zuber, Middle Amana, and Gus Miller, West Amana. Mr. Miller also will have charge at High Amana until a definite appointment is made there.

The store managers are: William F. Moershel, Amana; Carl Lippman, Homestead; Adam Kippenhan, Middle; William Foerstner, High; Hy Miller, West; Adam Ratzel, upper store at South Amana, and Ferdinand Ruff at the lower store. Managers of the three drugstores are: F.W. Miller, Amana; William August Moershel, Homestead; and A.F. Koch, Middle.

Peter Zimmerman has been appointed superintendent in charge of both woolen mills with offices at Amana. William Jeck is assistant in charge of the mill at Middle.

Three elevator and lumberyard businesses are operated. They will be managed by George Schuhmacher at Amana, William Gefaeller at Homestead, and Charles Ratzel Jr., South Amana.

Some of the smaller craftsmen's shops will be closed for the time being until definite arrangements can be worked out for them. There are several of these for cabinet making, rug-making, harness, shoe repair and various other purposes. August Franke will have charge of the cabinet shop at Amana.

Public schools are maintained and supported by taxation. The only taxpayer, however, is the society. Three-room schools are conducted at Amana and at Middle, and a two-room school at South. Each of the other towns has a one-room school. The schoolmasters are Ludvig Unglenk and J. Greichen at Amana; August Blechsmith and Rudolph Blechsmith at East; William C. Heinze, Fred A. Pitz and Martin V. Dickel at Middle; Fred Schaedlich at High; Paul E. Kellenberger at West; Emil Seifert and Adolph T. Berger at South, and Charles F. Fels at Homestead. A number of the older children also attend high school at society expense in nearby towns. Tentative plans have been made to establish a high school at one or more of the colonies.

The religious life of the society will continue as it was under the communistic system except that a separate corporation has been formed for that purpose. It is to be called The Amana Church Society. Articles of incorporation have been drawn up but are not yet filed....

Provision has been made in the articles of the new incorporation to take care of those who become needy through misfortune, sickness or accident.

The peace officers are those regularly elected by the township, namely justice of the peace, constable and health officer. One deputy sheriff of Iowa county lives at Homestead. He is John A. Kippenhan. A blanket bond for all employees who handle funds had been taken out so that in case of dishonesty the society will be protected and the offender dealt with by the bonding company.

Since the kitchens closed two weeks ago, an allowance or store credit of $1.10 a week per person has been made for food. Those who go on the payroll Monday will be dropped from the allowance list, but those who fail to find employment for awhile may continue to receive the allowance.

According to Mr. Barlow, there is an earnest desire on the part of each person to make the necessary adjustments and to fit into the new scheme so that speedy progress can be made toward the ultimate goal of a collective business enterprise that will pay substantial dividends.

Waste is Decreased, Life is Quickened Under New System in the Amanas

Waste Wanes as Amanas End Communism
Personal Initiative Stirs Among the Colonists

Des Moines Register, June 12, 1932
By Darrel Garwood

After a month's trial, this colony is, on the whole, delighted with results of the joint stock corporation into which it has merged after 85 years of communistic life.

The most obvious results have been:

1. A substantial decrease in the amount of waste, particularly of food.
2. A general quickening of activity, especially in farming the colony's 26,000 acres of land. All farm activity has been systematized under seven "agricultural managers." Fences have been rebuilt, general improvement initiated and plans for greater diversification of crops made.
3. A decrease in the cost of purchasing supplies and an efficient restocking of merchandising shops in the colony.
4. An increase in the amount of work done by each individual. Less "sickness" and less idling.
5. For many, a new outlook on life, occasioned by the desire to achieve higher positions and hence greater compensation in the colony.

"It is impossible as yet to give definite figures on the results of the plan," declared Arthur Barlow of Cedar Rapids, business manager of the corporation which began to function officially June 1, "but there are definite indications of what the results are to be."

Although there is no tabulation as to the decrease in the amount of food used by the colony, it has been found that only two-thirds as much milk and half as much bread is being taken from the stores. It is estimated that, through the elimination of waste, the colony is using a third less food than before.

"Under the old system, a colonist was permitted to take as much food and supplies from the common stores as he thought he would need, without charge," Dr. C.H. Herrman, a leader in the colony, explained. "Not knowing exactly how much he would need, he naturally took plenty, and much of it ended up in the chicken yards. Now that he must pay for the food, he is much more careful."

This same principle, it is believed, will apply to the use of other supplies. Extravagance in clothing is unknown among the colonists, stress being put on comfort, comeliness and propriety. But even with plain garments, there was a tendency at times to take more than was needed when there was no charge.

Agriculture has taken a new lease on life in the colony with the appointment of the seven managers, picked for their training and initiative. Those who were inclined to take life easy before now are striving for managerial positions or to remain on the payroll.

A system of requisitions and invoices initiated by Mr. Barlow is rapidly cutting down the cost of purchasing for the colony. Instead of allowing each shopkeeper to purchase at random what he seemed to need for his store, the purchasing has been centralized under one head, W.F. Marshall, and requisitions are made to him.

"I am certain that this plan will cause large savings to the colonists," Barlow stated Saturday.

"I have been impressing on the colonists that as time goes on we would need capable men to fill the more important positions in the colony," he continued. "The incentive to conduct a store efficiently and economically in order to retain the position as manager, together with the advantage of centralized buying, should cause great savings."

Compensations in the colony have not yet been adjusted, and at the present time, all are receiving the same amount of money from the general treasury. Since nothing ever is done hastily by these colonists who have dwelled east of Marengo since 1855, the adjustment of compensations will probably not be made until Jan. 1, 1933.

It is part of the scheme, however, to make such an adjustment, and already the colonists are working with renewed energy in the hope of being placed near the top of the payroll list.

Ice Harvest on the Iowa River, 1930s. Photograph by Rudolph Kellenberger.

This new spirit has caused an increase in the amount of work done by each individual and has made the members more determined to work, whether they are feeling their best or not. As the colony's own publication put it:

"We have several fine doctors in the colony, but Art Barlow has prevented more sickness than any of them." Barlow is treasurer and general manager of the business at Cedar Rapids.

Although the corporation did not officially begin its existence until June 1, the colony was conducted during May as though the new plan were in effect in order to make the change more gradual.

Everyone received compensation during May whether he was employed or not. Each member's compensations under both the old and new systems were calculated, and he was given the one which totaled the most.

Consequently the problem of unemployment is just beginning to oppress the colonists. Products of the colony's mills, factories and farm lands are bringing low prices, and with the individual output on the upgrade, it is a serious question as to how many will be left without work.

"Every effort will be made to provide employment for all members of the colony," Barlow said. "How far this will be possible, I do not know."

A plan to reduce the working day in the colony to as low as five hours, if necessary, in order to provide more jobs is being considered.

Amana Surrenders

The Country Home, July 1932
By Ben James

Communism is one of the oldest ways of life. Groups large and small have tried it in many parts of the world and in many periods of history. When life is hard, men are particularly likely to turn to it. Recently plans have been made for an agricultural colony in Minnesota, where unemployed families may live and work in an non-competitive society.

Out in Iowa, almost a century ago, the Amana Society started a communistic farm colony. For a hundred years it seemed to be a success. But now the colony has abandoned that method of life.

Why? Mr. James tells you in this graphic story of Amana—and the answer displays the strength and the weakness of communism.

The Editor

Within the year I have visited two contrasting camps of communism: Red Russia—creaking over the vague field of socialism in a clumsy, buoyant chase after the will-o'-the-wisp Utopia, and the Amana Colonies—a settlement of seven quaint villages scattered over 26,000 acres of Iowa farm land, where the fourteen hundred members are abandoning the tenets of communism which they have faithfully practiced for over three-quarters of a century.

In Russia I heard stories of hope and accomplishment. "We will banish poverty and insecurity from Russia," a commissar of Lenin's said to me. "And when we have abolished want, we shall have just begun to give a full life to our people."

But in Amana they have abolished want. Communism has given them all it can—yet it is not enough.

Just a week before the Amana Society voted to abandon the communistic system as a proved failure, I visited in the home of one of the members. It was a comfortable home—almost luxurious. We sat in his huge living-room, with the sun pouring through the windows onto a vast, hand-woven rag carpet. My host peered through rimless glasses perched on his thin nose, and his lips, drawn to a hard line by a life of self-suppression, gave his long, scholarly face an ascetic cast. He spoke evenly and quietly with a slight guttural German accent (for German is the language of the colony) as he pointed out the furnishings of the comfortable home. The heavy oak table and hulking chest of drawers, the modestly carved whatnot and long shelves lined with holy books had all been made by the village cabinetmaker with the care and precision of an artisan whose craft was his life. And the private rooms provided for each member of the family were furnished with colonial chairs, a four-poster bed—puffed high with feather ticks—and a kerosene lamp.

"You seem to have everything anyone would want," I said as we sipped old wine made by my host's grandfather. "Why change?"

"The more we have the more difficult it has become to get along under communism," he replied, evenly emphasizing the words with a nod of his brown, tufted head. "In the old days, when we all worked as a group and built up our community, each man saw himself better off by his own work. But since we have gained prosperity and struck a dead level, everyone says. 'Why work? We shall be cared for,' and now things are going downhill.

"Communism worked for us only when three factors prevailed: when we were absolutely isolated from the outside world; when the religious fervor was an urge strong enough to make people want to labor for the glory of the cause, and when each person saw himself gaining in material things by working for the group. But in recent years the world has come to us, religious enthusiasm has waned, and we are all comfortably fixed. Now there is decay. There is nothing left to work for—nothing that we want—except private wealth and privately owned goods such as radios, automobiles, etc."

Certainly the colony was not failing because of the lack of necessities of life. Evidences of these were abundant. Twenty-six thousand acres of fertile land on the banks of the Iowa River in the heart of the best farming area in the nation; factories; two woolen mills; slaughter houses; dairies; farm machinery; fat herds of cattle, sheep and hogs; improved roads, and seven villages, each with stores, hotels, bakeries and kitchens—these are included in the $3,000,000 properties owned by the colony. Eighty consecutive years, each showing a profit, are their record.

But about ten years ago there began a losing fight with the hard, gaudy world of modern things. The Amananites had hoped this world would go its way and leave them forgotten in their ancient peace. But it rushed upon them. Concrete was poured over mud roads that led to cities. The automobile and the tractor challenged their horses and oxen. In the nearby fields beacon lights of a transcontinental air route flashed. And the quiet night air that enveloped the pious villages was vibrant with radio jazz.

From the neighboring university, automobile loads of students, guided by their professors, came regularly to inspect the ways of communism. The young people clambered out of the cars and round-faced villagers watched the gay crowd from the sinful, capitalist city. Holy men, married too long to calico-clad women, stared at silk-stockinged college girls, and pretty drab-gowned maids of the colony glanced from beneath their bonnets at a football hero wandering down the dusty street.

Some of the younger people, eager for life, began to desert the colony. I talked with one of them in a city apartment a few days after my visit to the colony.

That morning she had sung in a metropolitan church. Her dark hair framed a Madonna-like face. Only her large, now well-kept hands showed the marks of twenty years of toil for her community. And a timidity bred by isolation told that the outside world was still strange to her. Her black afternoon gown was chic. A far cry it was from the peasant dress she had worn for twenty years. For until the last few years Amana women were uniformly gowned in a shirtwaist and skirt sewed together on a wide band. The voluminous skirt hung to the ground and obscured the woman's figure. In summer a sunbonnet with a long cap was the headdress, in winter a woolen hood.

"It was a tremendous decision for me to throw aside the odd garb I had worn through girlhood and leave the smug, sure life I had always known for that of a strange city," she told me. "But I was set upon becoming a singer. The notion of advanced musical training appeared absurd to the elders. For the only higher education open to anyone went to the few young people appointed by the elders for university training in professions needed by the group. The three doctors and three dentists serving the colony were educated at the expense of the community. Their services were, of course, free."

I offered her a cigarette.

"No, thanks. You see, my puritanical training has had its effect." She laughed. "It was not my objection to a normal standard or morals that provoked my rebellion. It was because the elders insisted upon an old-fashioned fanaticism that crushed normal life. Even my courtship and marriage, which happily was of my own making since I left the colony, would have been regulated."

Early in the life of the organization, marriage was frowned upon as an encroachment upon spiritual life. A terrifying warning to young men, "Fly from the association with women as a very dangerous magnet and magical fire," was thundered by a prophet.

Since a whole-hearted adherence to this notion threatened the existence of the colony beyond a generation, the idea was modified. Now a rule prevails that a man must be twenty-four to marry, and a woman twenty. After the betrothal the man is moved to a village away from his promised bride for a year. If at the end of that time his enthusiasm for the girl has not waned, the ceremony is performed, and by high spiritual living they re-establish themselves in the first brackets of the faith.

A childhood and youth of strict discipline designed to inculcate habits of hard work and to instill a notion that life is but a harsh period of probation for a chaste hereafter was the lot of those born in the colony in the past.

School six days a week was compulsory, with only one hour a day for play. After dismissal, there was work for every boy and girl until supper time—knitting and crocheting and rug-weaving for the girls, and jobs in the field and factory for the boys. In the evening there was prayer meeting and early bedtime, and the Sunday afternoon walk in the fields, the boys going one direction and the girls another, was the only diversion.

"Out of this severe life it was interesting to watch individual desires pop out from characters so thoroughly trained to suppress them," the woman who had abandoned the colony commented.

"Stories of New Year's Eve parties beyond our dull horizon filtered through to us young people," she recalled. "We decided to celebrate one December 31st in a bang-up fashion. We, of course, lacked many of the accepted requirements for such an event. But we carried out the idea. Immediately after prayer meeting we met at a remote barn at the edge of town. There we sat whispering around a smoky lantern, thrilled by our daring to undertake a gathering so unholy, and nervous beyond enjoyment lest we be caught. We considered the New Year as having arrived at nine-thirty and hurried to our homes with the pangs of troubled consciences solaced by the conviction that we could be like other people if given a chance."

Another story she told was significant of the eternal possessive urge and the desire of individuals to lift themselves out of the mass, even in such a successful community group as this.

"A group of women in the village used to come together to sew. But to give ourselves distinction, we decided to separate into a select unit. Secretly we determined to get buttons bearing insignia which would mark each of us as individuals, aloof from the others. But ten cents—the price of a button—was difficult to get, as all money was carefully paid to each family for the purchase of necessities only. Using one cent for purposes other than those decreed by the elders was unlawful, but at the expense of turbulent consciences we took this step. The sin done, it was easy to go on. We made a rule that anyone who stayed away for the meeting was to be fined a penny. The sums acquired from this source of revenue were kept surreptitiously independent of the community chests."

Such trivial infractions of rules were the forerunners of the revolution. A challenge to the elders' authority broke recently in the communal kitchens. All villages have several kitchens, each of which prepares and serves food to about forty diners. Each is in the charge of a woman arbitrarily delegated to the permanent position of kitchen manager, and the service of the meals and scullery work was done by young girls alternately assigned to the task. The members were seated at oblong tables—the men at one, the women at another—to "prevent silly conversations and trifling conduct."

All this was going on as usual until the order was issued a few months before the revolutionary ballot that breakfasts were to be prepared in the homes, due to insubordination on the part of the girls delegated for kitchen work. It was no easy task to be on duty at four-thirty in the morning, to build a fire in the vast iron-topped brick stove, prepare and serve a morning meal to forty people at six. And the last shimmering copper kettle would not be hung on its ceiling hook until nine in the evening. No pressure brought the workers there on time. Finally there was open rebellion, and entreaties and religious threats were of no avail.

The concession to the rebels had another repercussion that stirred latent individualism. A breakfast in the home with family alone was a pleasant enough affair. Why not other meals? Petitions for this privilege were forthcoming. Hard-pressed trustees yielded.

The quaint garb of old Germany, too, vanished into the modern air as the mutineers gained courage. In the community drugstore in one of the villages I saw girls in sports clothes that reflected the influence of current mail-order catalogs. Were the elders to bar them from a series of church services for such frivolous practice, the young ones would say: "We've had enough of church every day. A vacation from it would be a treat. We've learned that there is no relation between religion and face powder." And despite ecclesiastic frowns upon the machine age, schoolboys tumbled into the old apothecary shop with aviators' helmets for caps.

In the village bakery where the tremendous round loaves that supply the town are baked, I heard the growl of rising discontent on the eve of the change to capitalism. The baker, who was raking the coals from the huge oven preparatory to putting in the loaves, dropped his work and commenced at once to harangue the local professional man who was guiding me through the town.

"Look how the bread was yesterday," growled the baker, holding out a cracked loaf. "And see today's sponge," he continued, tossing open the lid of a bin. "It is not good, and it is not my fault. Look at the flour I get from the mill."

"And the miller says he is not to blame," replied my discouraged companion. "In fact, no one ever seems to be to blame for anything that goes wrong."

Turning to me he shrugged his shoulders. "How can you fix responsibility under this system?"

As we passed the meetinghouse, a pleasant old man smiled a greeting that lighted up his fat, weather-beaten face.

"That man is an elder," said the villager. "The elders have difficult jobs these days."

While we walked through the village, my host explained the powers of the elders and the constitution under which they had operated since coming to Iowa.

"No one receives wages. Those men there," he said, waving his hand in the direction of the workers repairing a road, "get no less than the doctor. Food and rent are free. The allotment of money is determined by the living requirements of the individual.

"And every member of the colony," he said, shaking his head hopelessly, "is assigned his or her job by the elders. This way of putting our people to work has caused lots of trouble. The boy down here sawing wood wants to be a dentist, but the elders chose a young fellow of the same age to go to the university. Both of the boys are bright youngsters; both could be dentists. But the man on the woodpile stood no chance."

A week after this conversation, the colony came to the conclusion that responsibility under such a system could not be fixed. Eighty percent of the colony voted to abandon communism and incorporate under a capitalistic plan, pay wages, allow each individual free use of the money he earns, and a right to compete for an occupation.

Instead of a model communal colony that the world has watched as the oldest one in existence, the eyes of the agricultural world may center again on Amana, this time to see it as a corporation farm that combines manufacture with large-scale production of its own raw materials.

It was the young and middle-aged members who brought about the change. The old men and women cannot favor the drastic leap into the strange world. Despite the fact that the new plan ensured complete care for the old and infirm, they see it as an ungodly decision. Peace and simple security, they believe, have been traded for the bitter struggle of precarious competition. And quiet lives of labor and prayer have been bartered for the pleasures of the machine age.

Traces Progress of Amana Colonies

Business Manager of Corporation Cites Cooperative Spirit in Which Members Accept Change

Cedar Rapids Gazette, July 20, 1932

The progress of the Amana colonies from their origin in 1714 as the Ebenezer colonies in Germany through their settlement as a communistic group in Buffalo, N.Y., (1844) and their migration in 1854 to Iowa, to their present transition into a corporation, was outlined to the Kiwanis club Wednesday noon by Arthur A. Barlow, business manager of the Amana corporation.

Speaking of the way in which the colonists had accepted their new organization Mr. Barlow said that in spite of the fact that these people had spent their whole lives without a unit of measuring work, they now are responding to the whistle, punching the timeclock and checking off hours in the field with a fine spirit of cooperation.

He mentioned the fact that their wages really amount to more than 10 cents an hour since their rent is free and their commodities are obtained at cost during this transitional year.

Had To Get Used To Money

The habit of exchanging money, which has become so common to most Americans, was something which required time for the Amanas. Older people left the stores fondling their change and trying to become accustomed to the feel of it.

Briefly Mr. Barlow outlined the plan of the incorporation, which involved the separation of the business from the church. Church properties, including churches, schools and cemeteries, are to be managed by the school board. The business side of the project involved an appraisal of the property with its aggregate pro-rated to members in the form of prior distributive shares in lieu of services rendered. Medical and dental services are still furnished free to all members, a holdover of the old communism.

154

Transition Big Problem

An idea of the many problems that this transition involves was given the audience in a series of figures concerning the colony—its 26,000 acres of land with 4,500 acres in crops, 2,000 head of cattle, 300 head of hogs, and so on down the line.

Mr. Barlow began his talk with a resumé of the history of the colonies, of their beginnings as the Community of True Inspiration under the direction of a clergyman and a clergyman's son, whose new creed did away with the worldly aspects of the older religion. Looking for a land more tolerant to religion, 800 of the colonists settled on 10,000 acres of land near Buffalo, where they established mills and tanneries. In search of quietness and further removal from the worldly the group came to Iowa in 1854 where they took their name from the Bible, a title meaning "to remain true."

Pointing out the unusual characteristics of the colonies which attract the interest of outsiders Mr. Barlow mentioned the uniformity of their houses, dress and conveniences; the lack of hurry and hustle; the unusual abilities of different members to work out their own problems without instruction and facilities; the splendid hobbies they had developed; the love of nature that they teach.

Brides continued to wear the traditional black Amana church attire at their weddings for several years after the Great Change. Photograph shows Erma Schanz and Rudolph Kellenberger holding their church books on their wedding day, Sept. 30, 1933.

Making of Rag Carpets

Is Both an Art and a Tradition in Amana

Homes are Brightened

Each colony has its weaver and housewives save everything that can be used for material.

Cedar Rapids Gazette, July 20, 1932

By Adeline Taylor

Amana lawns are carpeted with flowers. Amana floors are covered with stripes. Gay and gray stripes, twisted and straight stripes, narrow and wide stripes, symmetrical and one-side stripes, cotton and woolen stripes, multi-colored and single-shaded stripes.

Every room of every house of every colony has a complete change of stripes. Walking in the yard or through the kitchen of an Amana home, one steps on brilliance that stands out in vivid contrast against the somber grayness of the unpainted frame buildings.

When the Amanans first settled in the Iowa hills some ninety years ago as a communistic community, which has been recently changed into a corporation, they had nothing but bare floors in their homes, some of them covered with sand. It was the industrious and thrifty housewives who changed all that. They made the transformation with rags. And even to this day, the floors are covered with rags.

Nothing is ever thrown away. Old coats, old suits, old shirts, old socks, old sheets, old sweaters, old tablecloths—everything is stored until harvest is over and quiet winter months set in. Then all the discarded remnants are sorted out, laundered, cut into narrow strips, sewed end to end, and wound into skeins.

In order not to make all this work too tedious, the women get together for carpeting bees. Every other year or so, a housewife notices that the carpets in the front room are beginning to look worn, so she issues her invitation and the neighborhood turns out with their best thimbles and gossip to spend the afternoon drinking coffee and sewing carpet rags.

The next step in the re-creation of rags to stripes is that of dyeing, which takes place in the mills at Middle Amana. Cotton rags are dyed tan and brown for the striped background; woolen rags are turned into bright blues and crimsons and purples for the pattern stripes. Wound into balls, the rags next visit the village weaver.

Weaving is not yet a lost art in the Amanas. Each colony has its weaver, the veteran of whom is 75-year-old Louis Hess of East Amana. He is the only one of this trade left in the community still using a hand loom. In and out he throws the bobbins, keeping accurate check by memory of how many rows of blue and black and red and green each housewife has ordered for her particular floor covering.

In the house where Mr. Hess lives are many and varied examples of both carpets and rugs. Rag carpets cover the floors and rag rugs ornament the carpets in Amana homes.

The cream of the rag supply is used in rugs—knitted, crocheted, woven, tied, hooked and braided rugs. Dorothy Schuerer, Mr. Hess' granddaughter, is a past master at tied rugs. She takes an old sock, sweater sleeve or shawl and unravels the knitting, looping the curly yarn back and forth until she has an egg-sized ball, then ties it and starts on another. These balls sewed in pattern form on burlap make as lovely and deep-napped a rug as ever you stepped on.

Others cut the rags into tiny strips about an inch long and a quarter as wide, knitting the snips of color into flowered patterns that last for centuries. At least, they last for one century because there are some chair covers in the colonies made that many years ago.

Some of the handcraft artists prefer to knit their rugs from yarn instead of rags. All these rugs are made from separate knitted squares put together in afghan fashion. Some of the best examples of these are to be found in Homestead, in the Eichacker and Selzer homes. Next to the room where a large knitted rug made by Mrs. Louisa Selzer covers the floors is a lovely display of hooked rugs made by Mrs. Henrietta Selzer.

There are some homes where this form of rug handcraft has developed many offspring. It is a joy, for example, to visit with Mrs. Louis Rettig in Middle Amana and admire her handwork even though she cannot speak a word of English. Mrs. Rettig must have discovered the secret of eternal youth long ago, for although she is more than sixty years old, her small, round face is untouched by lines of worry and weariness. Her white hair braided in a coronet around her head and her white teeth that sparkle when she smiles stand out in contrast to her smooth skin bronzed by many sunny days in the gardens. And her eyes are blue—deep, bright, shining blue that reflect the animated energy which has conceived the boxes full of handwork that fill a cupboard in her house.

Making flowers grow in summertime was not enough to satisfy Mrs. Rettig's hunger for creating beauty, so she makes them in the winter. She makes them from seed—seeds of flower and weeds, pits from fruit and grains from the field. A handful of rice she can turn into a lovely star-shaped blossom, and with a cup of corn she can make a bouquet of brown-eyed susans. Hanging in her sitting room is a picture she made from these seed-petalled flowers.

When she isn't increasing her seed garden during the spare hours of winter, she is crocheting additions to her miniature menagerie. That menagerie includes tiny Easter bunnies sitting on nests of bright-colored crocheted eggs; men leading bears on yard chains; hens and chicks and ducks and ducklings; goats standing about two inches high and complete from their hooves to their whiskers.

It's a hobby with Mrs. Rettig, a hobby that started with the colony hobby of making rugs. She has had no art training, nor has she had any patterns to work by. It's just a matter of an urge to create and an originality of expression.

Rugs made yesterday lie on Amana carpets, side by side with rugs made fifty, sixty, seventy and eighty years ago. And there is not much difference between the handwork of grandmother and granddaughter. Both have chosen for their original designs the flowers with which they are so familiar. Both have displayed the accurate craftsmanship of trained and patient fingers.

The best way to pick out the rugs and carpets of long ago, however, is to look for the old Amana prints in their patterns. Time was when Amana women's dresses were made only from harsh and heavy prints with dark blue backgrounds broken by tiny white patterns. The iron-like threads were uncomfortable for wearing apparel but serviceable for rugs. Hundreds of footsteps have tramped over them without making an impression.

These Amana women have made an art out of economy, a rainbow out of rags, a tradition out of industry....In Amana you identify a colony by the stripes on which they walk.

Sisters Run South Amana Hotels Where Guests of Far Lands Eat Apple Fritters

Two Women Have Been in Hotel Business for 48 Years but Never Yet Used Can Opener.

Cedar Rapids Gazette, July 31, 1932
By Adeline Taylor

No matter how you cut it, it's still spinach. Nevertheless, it is only the cut of the spinach that has been changed at the famous South Amana hotels since the colonists became a corporation. The managers should be able to speak authoritatively on that subject for they have been in the hotel business at Amana for just short two years of half a century. They are sisters—the two sweetest, white-haired sisters you ever met—by the name of Mrs. Lizzie Siegel and Miss Emma Zierold.

To clear up this spinach matter—when the colonists were communists and ate in kitchens, they took their spinach chopped. But more recently the spinach has been prepared in the original leaf form, in which condition it is known as Barlow spinach. (Arthur Barlow of Cedar Rapids is the business manager of the corporation.) Every morning that there is spinach on the menu the hotel girls ask Aunt Emma—or Aunt Lizzie—"Is it to be colony spinach or Barlow spinach today?" But even spinach is good in the Amana hotels, for, whether it's the colony or Barlow variety, it never comes out of cans. In fact, one doubts if either sister would know how to use a can opener if she saw one. All the fruits and vegetables served on these hotel tables grow in gardens, not in tins. Even in the winter they are grown in gardens—cellar gardens.

Lots of the vegetables are pulled right out by their roots in the fall and transplanted in boxes of dirt in the cellars of the South Amana hotels. Others are stored in sand. And what won't keep that way is put up in jars for winter. The preserving season has barely started, but already Mrs. Siegel has 200 quarts of pickled beets and 300 quarts of tomatoes on her shelves.

Pickled beets are one of the highlights of the South Amana menus.

159

If a guest does not eat—well, around twenty-five of them at a meal—the sister cooks feel rather slighted. If you don't like pickled beets, however, you can partake of pickled celery hearts. And who doesn't like them has grown up without a properly cultivated palate. They're a delicacy such as only Amanans can perfect.

All these are mere preliminaries, however, to the real treat of the repast. That is apple fritters. Never a meal goes by anymore without apple fritters. The sisters have given up trying to sneak through setting a table without them. When someone from Iowa City or Cedar Rapids or Marengo calls up and says:

"We have guests from Chicago. Make reservations for twelve for dinner."

They ask, "What would you like to eat?"

The answer invariably is, "Oh, just apple fritters."

They serve a lot more than that, of course, but none of it is enjoyed if it is not accompanied by apple fritters.

"When did you learn to make apple fritters?" we asked the sisters.

But they can't remember. They grew up cooking, and they just can't think back as far as a day when they didn't know how.

The recipe for the famous apple fritters is not secret. Here it is—enough to satisfy six people.

2 cups flour	Level teaspoon of soda
1/3 cup sugar	Pinch of salt
2 eggs	1/2 cup sweet milk
1/2 cup buttermilk	4 sliced apples

Break eggs into sifted salt, sugar and flour. Add buttermilk with soda. Stir in apple. Dip tablespoons of dough in deep skillet of hot lard and fry until brown.

That's the recipe, but that's not a promise that your fritters will taste as good as the ones do at Amana. Those who have tried it out say that they never taste the same at home as they do at the colony tables.

"Don't they ever turn out wrong?" we asked Aunt Lizzie.

"No," she shook her head, "never."

"Haven't you ever had a kitchen tragedy?" we insisted.

Well, it took Mrs. Siegel a long time to think up one, but finally it was remembered. The only tragedy—and it was only a near-tragedy at that—occurred when she was hastily called early one morning to the home of a relative where a blessed event was about to occur. Aunt Lizzie was in the midst of mixing up a coffee cake. Hurriedly she got the dough ready, put it aside to rise and arrived at the scene on time. But just as they were about to welcome the stork, she remembered something. Horrors! She had forgotten the salt! There were no telephones then with which to correct the error. But that didn't daunt Aunt Lizzie. She hunted out a young member of the family, wrote a note and dispatched word to the neighboring kitchen by the small messenger. So it all turned out all right, and neither the coffee cake nor the new arrival had to suffer.

It was in 1884 that the hotel at Upper South Amana was erected, at which time both sisters began to learn the hotel business. In 1897 Mrs. Siegel went to Lower South and left the neighboring hotel entirely to her sister. When she first came to Lower South the yard, which is now a smooth, shaded lawn, was one great sunny stretch of vegetable garden. She and her husband spread the seed and planted the trees which have transformed it. And for a real vista which feeds your soul in the same satisfying way that those apple fritters do, stroll through the back yard of the hotel at Upper South and look far out over the fields to the wooded hills in the distance.

The hotel sisters came to the Amanas from Ohio when Aunt Lizzie was 14 and Aunt Emma was 12. Now they are 67 and 65 years old. Each parts her hair in the center, combs it in smooth white wings that frame her kind and understanding face. Each wears a crisp cotton house dress with the same quaint kind of print. Each covers her gown with a prim, piped apron. And each, I'm sure, is as hospitable a hostess as any of their guests registered from Germany, England, Japan and many of these United States has ever met.

From the *Amana News Bulletin,*
Vol. I, Amana, Ia., Thurs., Sept. 12, 1932, No. 20

"The following shops are for sale: Cabinet shops at Middle and East, Cooper shop at Middle, Tin shop at Amana. Bids should be in not later than Oct. 1, 1932."

Excerpts from

Amanas as Their Neighbors See Them — Since the Recent Changes to Modernism

The Iowa Publisher and the *Bulletin of the Iowa Press Association,* Vol. 4, November, 1932, No. 11

By Roland A. White

The Amanas until recently had no publications of their own, no records except official documents and private keepsakes and church records. In them is the story distilled and condensed; the story of transition as a living process is best set down in black and white by neighboring newspapers—often from correspondence sent by Amana colonists themselves....

An Iowa daily commented Feb. 3 that "The voluntary termination of the Amana experiment...augurs no happy future for the Russian venture"—when actually Amana has more nearly resembled the religious oligarchy of Puritan New England and when the social revolution of Amana will take advantage of the same modern machinery which is so great an asset to Soviet Russia.

...In the *Marengo Pioneer-Republican* that week one of the more influential of the 930 colony voters asserted that "Our organization will no longer be communistic; it is not capitalistic nor yet co-operative but we have tried to select the best from all three."

...March 10 found the *Cedar Rapids Gazette*...with an underline explaining that colony wives were about to become housewives at home instead of kitchen servants of the community. "...husbands, who have not tasted their wives' cooking in two decades of married life together, will be given an opportunity to judge their culinary arts."

April 7 saw the first art exhibit at the Amanas in 76 years of their history in Iowa, with Carl Flick of West Amana exhibiting his paintings of colony scenes at the Homestead hotel, with the village's Welfare club and Artist Grant Wood of Cedar Rapids aiding.

...Articles of incorporation for the new plan filed at Marengo May 17, may not have been as significant as the appearance May 26 of a newspaper display advertisement in that town's weekly paper. Meal time schedules and prices at four Amana hotels were announced....

Some typical items from the correspondence during June-September reveal....

"Old Fritz, veteran livery horse, died last week. Fritz, since his 7th year, has faithfully served in transferring passengers and the United States mail between the two local (South Amana, Rock Island, Milwaukee & St. Paul) railroad stations, besides performing other duties. During the last few years, he was allowed to roam in the timber on account of trucks being installed and his services were no longer needed.... He was about 27 years old."

"High Amana lost their valuable herd bull last week, when it got sick and died about four hours later. It was a very beautiful roan shorthorn."

Much more could be told—how Amana residents got their first driver's licenses this summer, and how they have yet to experience paying taxes....how Amana cooperation on vegetables made possible again the Iowa county farm products booth's sweepstakes victory at the State Fair; how Amana farm managers decided to lime their fields; how unemployment as a problem has superseded that of parasites; how filling stations have sprung up;...how dress has become modern and American.

From *Wallace's Farmer* for July 9: "We believe the new Amana Society can be of tremendous significance to the people of the United States during the next twenty years. Under the new set-up, it furnishes a sociological and economic laboratory which may point the way out of some of our difficulties."

Ray Anderson, *Cedar Rapids Gazette* farm editor, deserves the last quoted word—from his "FENCE DRIFT caught in the woven wire" for Sept. 16: "Homes, / Medievally massive, / Unpainted but / Festooned with laden vine, / Midst groaning pear trees, apples. / Gardens. / Silhouettes at / Moonlit eventide / Any of the Amana villages / As night draws near. / Peace and plenty, / Comfort. / Fewer grander scenes ever visioned. / Homes."

Transition Period Will End Jan. 1

Employment for all is expected under corporation plan; conferences held in all 7 colonies.

Cedar Rapids Gazette, December 21, 1932

...What about the "transition period" between communism and a cooperative corporation? Will it terminate Jan. 1 as anticipated when put into effect last June? How do living conditions and employment compare with "outside?"

These and other questions of mutual concern were discussed with the members during the series of meetings by Dr. Henry G. Moershel, president of the Amana Society; Peter Stuck, secretary; Arthur Barlow, business manager; and Jake Roemig, assistant business manager.

The transition period will end New Year's Day as scheduled, and the corporation will start 1933 in sound financial condition with all persons employed and the morale of the member-stockholders on a high plane, the executives declare.

Wage scales will be altered slightly upward, varying in degree with the value of the service. This upward trend will not be as definite as hoped, due to the fact that "outside economic conditions" act as a deterrent to the various businesses conducted at the Amanas.

The enterprise as a whole, however, shows a fair profit for operations during the transition period...The woolen mills operated several weeks with double shifts from 6:30 a.m. until 10 p.m. Recently mill employees went on a ten-hour basis while some of them were released to help with the ice harvest which is in full swing just now. All available hands have been busy on the lake and ponds and in the several ice houses this week. The ice is of high quality, clear and more than a foot thick. Many independent farmers of the community have been buying and hauling ice from the colonies.

Double shifts will be resumed at the woolen mills when the ice harvest is completed, says Peter Zimmerman, superintendent. Despite full production during the fall and early winter, no surplus stocks of woolen goods have accumulated, and constant orders indicate future production will be moved.

No Unemployment at Amana Colonies: Mills Work Double Shift

Church Club Hears Success of New Plan
Dr. C.F. Noe Tells of Transition Period Now Under Way at Amanas

Iowa City Press-Citizen, December 21, 1932

At the close of the transition period in the change from a communistic society to a joint-stock corporation, the members of the Amana colonies are hopeful of the success of the plan in the future, Dr. C.F. Noe, a member of the colonies, told the Unitarian Men's Club at a meeting Tuesday evening.

Until last June 1, the society was operating share and share alike among the members, and that same spirit was carried over into the new corporation plan. For the last six months, there has been no unemployment in the colonies, Doctor Noe said, and the members, by working the colony mills, its fields and other industries have been able to live comfortably during the transition period.

One of the most hopeful manifestations of the new plan, Doctor Noe said, was the ability of the new organization to operate without financial loss and have no unemployment. Profits have been cut in order to keep everyone at work. For the first time since the World War, the mills are being operated on a double shift. Each worker in the colonies is paid 10 cents an hour at the present time.

"We are not operating at a profit," Doctor Noe said, "but we are not losing money and there is no suffering, everyone is living comfortably. The problem for the future will be the willingness of the members to continue to carry sacrifices, which I believe they will do."

Doctor Noe paid tribute to Mr. Arthur Barlow, the business manager of the colonies, for the success of the plan to date. Mr. Barlow, an outsider to the colonies, was called in to aid the new organization. The speaker related that the manager has centralized the government, installed a system, and has centralized the management of the farms, mills, stores and other industries.

Each of the seven villages has its store manager, bakery manager, meat market manager, etc., Doctor Noe related, and the managers confer each week with Mr. Barlow, as do the farm managers and others. The main office receives regular reports of all business.

Doctor Noe said there was no anxiety for the future as the members know their wants will be supplied in old age and there is no suffering from lack of medical or dental care, for both are furnished to stockholders free of charge.

In addition to working for the 10 cents an hour, the society members will share the profits of the corporation, if any, the speaker stated. The older members hold large portions of stock, because distribution of the prior share was made chiefly on a basis of years of service in the colony. Doctor Noe said that the society does not plan to continue on a basis of 10 cents an hour uniform salaries. After the first of the year, a gradual readjustment looking toward the payment of wages in proportion to the individual member's value to the society will be inaugurated.

Among some of the so-called evils of the former organization which have been eliminated in the new, mentioned by Doctor Noe, include laxity in performance of duties, waste of the colony's food and supplies, inefficiency in purchasing, and the general disorganization, doing away with the "drones" and operating on the slogan, "You can't live unless you work."

Mr. Barlow is holding a series of meetings in the villages at the present time, the speaker said, to get a general idea of conditions. The colonies issue a weekly corporation news bulletin which contains the reports of the business manager.

The change in organization is not a socialistic or an economic experiment, the speaker said, but aims to follow in the steps of the forefathers, no change being made in the deep seated religion of the colonies.

Christmas Spirit Ideal in Amana Colonies: Santa Visits Every Child

Week of Celebration Begun Last Night at Homestead with Yule Program in Old Wine Cellar

Cedar Rapids Gazette, December 1932
By Adeline Taylor

Do you know where Santa Claus was last evening? In a Homestead wine cellar at the Amana colonies—the sly old scamp. But instead of kegs of rare old fermented grapes, he found benches lined with expectant youngsters. Nor was he surprised, for that is exactly what has greeted him in the wine cellar for the last eight years....where the Homestead Welfare Club holds it annual Christmas celebration.

There are narrow lanes that wind among the snow-roofed gray houses of the village of Homestead at this season, and at the end of one of them are two big wooden doors that unlatch, swing open and let the visitor down the stone steps to the low-ceilinged cellar where the spirits were once stored—not Christmas spirits either.

The stories that must have been spun 'round a candlelit table in that dark musty room! Ghosts of yesteryear were surely surprised the first time they found a stage built in the corner of their hideout, fir trees dripping silver icicles on the walls, and wreaths of cedar strong with colored lights overhead. But they have probably become accustomed to it by now. No doubt they smile to see their grandsons work so hard to make the gas motor in an adjoining building furnish current for the electric lights when they had but to strike a match to the candle wick—and they're probably glad to hear pine logs crackling again in the stoves.

It takes many weeks to prepare for these Homestead celebrations. The walls that hem the stage are prepared; dressing rooms are curtained off; spotlights are arranged to give sun and moon effects; plays are rehearsed, carols practiced—so busy is the wine cellar that the shades must hide their faces in shame to see so much strenuous activity in their lazy haunt.

Santa Claus always climaxes the evening's activities—a Santa Claus so big and fat and jolly that they sent a miniature St. Nick around to all the children's homes the first part of the week to warn them about Santa's expansive rotundity and explain to them that he needs lots of space to carry around all his Christmas cheer. This is so there will be no frightened tears from those youngsters celebrating their initial Christmas and meeting Santa for the first time.

The good old saint never waits until Christmas Eve to visit the Amanas; he starts his nightly visits several days beforehand to be sure that the boys and girls are good enough to warrant receiving the products of his toy shop labors. Never did you see such angelic children as these Amananites are during probation period. About a week before Christmas they set their shoes outside their bedroom doors, and, if in the morning they find some candy or nuts in the toes, they know that Santa has begun his holiday touring.

On Christmas Eve all the children of the family gather in the room next to the parlor where the tree is being trimmed, a room darkened so they can watch the lights shine through the cracks and keyhole and wait breathlessly for the bell that tells them they may enter. All the gifts and toys are piled near the tree—a tree which has a tiny manger scene built beneath it—and they spend the evening unwrapping packages, singing songs and telling Christmas stories.

This Christmas Eve marks the climax of the holiday celebrations, for Christmas itself is a day of devotion. Three church services are held—morning, afternoon and night—and except for the noonday meal, with a table groaning under its holiday dishes, there is no sign of the rollicking gaiety that marks the pre-Christmas festivities.

This first Yuletide spent as a corporation rather than a communism will also be the first one for which each family has cooked its own Christmas dinner. Formerly all the food was prepared in the community kitchens. Roast goose will occupy the position of honor on almost every table—a goose stuffed with mashed potatoes in which the giblets have been ground. And never a Christmas goes by without stollen on the table, a German pastry filled with almonds, citron, currants, raisins and all the other things we put in our fruit cakes, but raised with yeast and baked like bread.

How would you like to be preparing a Christmas dinner for a family of sixteen? That number, which will gather around the John Eichacher table Christmas noon, represents the average size of the groups that will assemble in the colonies next Sunday noon, for family trees have not yet forced their roots over wide territories in this group of villages.

Christmas cooking starts several weeks ahead of time with the baking of the Christmas cookies. Mrs. Eichacher baked twenty dozen of them from seven different recipes, all tested out centuries ago by great-great-grandmothers back in Germany. There are stars, circles, bars, and animals, and all kinds of fancy shapes. Some are made from honey, some flavored with anise, some filled with nuts and citron, some so soft they melt in your mouth, some crisp and crunchy, some frosted, some sugar-sprinkled. Twenty dozen sounds like an enormous lot of cookies until you taste Mrs. Eichacher's. Then you wonder how they last as long as they do.

Christmas presents are many of them handmade in the colonies, and therefore, doubly precious. Rugs are woven in the typical Amana striped way; bed-coverings are quilted in tiny stitched designs; doll furniture is carved from bits of wood, and games are made. All of them meaning more than store-made presents because they represent the work of loving hands.

We can think of no place where the Christmas spirit so nearly approaches the ideal than in the Amana colonies. There will be no family there a week from today without a Christmas dinner, no home where Santa has not visited, no child whose shoe has not been filled with candy. The season is simply celebrated; the day is sacredly kept.

Christmas card from the Museum of Amana History's collection

New Chapter in Life of Amana Colonists Begins with New Year

Des Moines Register, January 1, 1933

With the new year begins the writing of a new page in the history of the Amana Colonies, which are as foreign to their Iowa surroundings as a cinder in your eye.

Members of the society take their final step from communal existence to corporate ownership of their $2,500,000 worth of property.

The initial step was taken June 1, when the new stock corporation was formed. The six months since have been a transition period in which members gradually have become accustomed to the change.

Today the members will leave the old order behind formally to enter the new era.

For three quarters of a century preceding June 1, no money changed hands among the residents of this communal cloister. Necessities of life were provided by the society and credits for additional requirements were issued to the members. These credits were good at the community stores where purchases were charged against them.

With the opening of the transition period, members of the society had their first experiences in handling legal money, making change and keeping individual cash and credit accounts.

The credit slips issued by the society were made payable in cash. Any member has been able to draw cash, in sums of not less than $5, against his credit at the store in the community in which he lives.

There is no bank in any of the Amana villages, and there will be none after the first of the year. The eight stores in the seven villages were owned by the old society and continue to be owned by the new corporation.

The credit accounts are kept at the central office in the store here. The cash paid out and received by the eight stores is returned to the general office, and the cash balance is kept in an outside depository bank.

During the transition period the communal principle of equality of contribution of all members to the common good has been maintained to the extent that each has received equal credit for his labor, whether he is a gardener or superintendent of a mill.

Families have continued to live rent-free in the same society-owned homes they occupied before; their purchases from the village stores have been made at cost, and all members employed have received 10 cents an hour in wages.

The most visible change made last summer when the colonists transferred from communal to corporate management was abandonment of the community kitchens in which members ate their meals.

When each family began to prepare its own meals, however, its purchase continued practically on a community basis.

Under the new order, the corporation will operate much as any other corporation.

Families will own or rent their own houses, but will not be able to obtain individual title to farms. The wages paid will be graduated according to the ability and value of the workers. The farms and the industries will be owned and operated by the corporation.

Every member of the old communal society, besides free board and dwelling and support and care secured to him in old age, sickness and infirmity, was entitled out of the common fund to an annual sum of maintenance for his family and relations.

Annual allowances were fixed by the trustees for each member. Members had no share in the income and profits in the common fund.

Every member of the new corporation owns one share of common stock and additional shares allotted on the basis of length of membership in the old society. Each, therefore, in exchange for the benefits of the communal society has received stock in a new corporation. The shares in addition the common, called prior distributive shares, are entitled to seven percent annual dividends, if the corporation earns them.

The Class A common stock is the voting stock in the corporation. No stockholder may cast more than one vote. The prior distributive shares were issued on the following basis:

After deductions of debts, a sum for minors, and after setting aside a surplus from the net assets of the corporation, the remainder was divided by the total years of service of all the members to obtain the value of one year of service.

Each member was issued one prior distributive share for each total year of service and scrip for fractional years.

The prior distributive shares are valued at $65 each. A year of service, based on the net assets and the total years of service of all members, was computed at $65. The par value of the prior distributive shares is $50, with the remaining $15 representing surplus.

The scrip is convertible into prior distributive shares upon payment of the balance above the face value of the scrip. For instance, a member receiving $40 in scrip could obtain a share by paying $25. The scrip is not entitled to dividends.

Members are buying their houses by turning in their stock. If they haven't bought their houses by today, or started negotiations with the officers to buy them, members will have to pay rent to the corporation.

Both the purchase value and the rental value are determined by the appraised valuation of the property. The appraisal was made for the executive council at the time the stock issue was approved.

Peter Stuck, secretary of the corporation, said the houses are appraised at from as low as $200 to as high as $1,500.

Multiple houses may be purchased by arrangement between the present occupants. Rent for those who do not buy will be 1-1/2 percent of the appraised value a month, Mr. Stuck said.

After today, Secretary Stuck said, the personnel of the farms and industries in the colonies will continue about as it is.

Men in responsible places will receive a slight increase in pay. The directors and officers, who have been receiving the same pay as other members, will be paid—the directors for attending meetings and the officers salaries.

The directors control the personnel through the business manager. There are 13 directors, one from each of the seven villages and six at large. The terms of seven directors expire in February 1933, and the terms of the other six expire in February 1934.

The business manager is Arthur Barlow of Cedar Rapids, a former banking examiner for the Minnesota State Banking Department, who devotes half-time to his business in Cedar Rapids and half-time to the Amana Society. In the mornings, Mr. Barlow acts as treasurer and general manager of the Shores-Mueller Co., manufacturing chemists in Cedar Rapids, and in the afternoons, he is in his office at Amana.

All the employees of the general office in Amana are members of the society.

The society kept its same name, Amana Society, when it changed from its old constitution under the chapter governing non-pecuniary profit organizations to a corporation for pecuniary profit. Barlow is not a member of the society. He receives a salary of $5,000 a year.

The total resources of the society are a little more than $2,000,000, Mr. Barlow said. The authorized capital stock is $2,078,300. Of this stock, but $1,559,700 has been issued, Mr. Stuck said.

The outstanding stock is as follows, he said: Class A common stock, $46,850; Prior distribute shares, $1,494,350; Scrip, $18,500.

The church property, including cemeteries, has been transferred to a separate corporation known as the Amana Church Society.

The society maintains three physicians and one dentist to provide free medical and dental care for the holders of Class A common stock and their immediate dependents. Medicines and dental supplies are not free, except that the society provides expensive serums beyond the means of members in emergencies.

The board of directors is authorized to provide for giving aid to the holders of Class A common stock or their immediate dependents who, through misfortune, sickness or old age, are in want or suffering, and it may contribute to the Amana Church Society....

Dr. Henry G. Moerschel, Homestead, is president of the society. The other officers are Gustav Miller, West, vice president; Peter Stuck, Amana, secretary; and William W. Moerschel, Amana, treasurer.

The new board of directors will choose officers for the new year after the seven whose terms expire in February are elected Feb. 6.

Directors whose terms expire in 1933 are Peter C. Zimmerman, Amana; Adolph Heinemann, Middle; Henry Bendorf, High; Gustav Miller, West; Theodore Setzer, South Amana; Fred Marz, Homestead; and Richard Schaefer, Amana.

The holdover directors are William F. Moerschel, Amana; Dr. Charles F. Noe, Amana; Peter Stuck, Amana; Jacob Roemig, Amana; Henry G. Moerschel, Homestead; and Louis Selzer, Homestead.

"Perfect" Communistic Colony Drops Doctrines for Capitalistic Plan

Pasadena Post, January 17, 1933

The communistic Amana Colonies have turned capitalistic and are using real money as local exchange for the first time in their seventy-five years of existence....Sociologists and economists cited the colonies as the world's most perfect example of communistic success.

It was a strange mingling of the old and the new that finally broke the communistic system. Youths introduced to capitalism became restless when there was no jingle of money in their pockets after a week's work....

Amana Turns to Coin

Chicago Journal of Commerce, January 18, 1933

As the individualist bulwarks of American rural life are being turned by their agitating leaders more and more clearly toward state socialism through prospective doles, one Middle West community which has lived the communist life since back in the fifties (1850s) turned the new year with a change to a thorough capitalistic system. The Amana religious colony near Cedar Rapids, Iowa, has been experiencing disaffection from the old ideas for several years as a main highway built to ribbon through the heart of the community and a transcontinental airline zoomed overhead. The disaffection has not been religious, however; the colonists, both old and young, have found that the commune does not give the financial satisfaction to the communicants so necessary to make them stay with the group in the coming, even more modern years.

So money—coin of the realm, no round-robin currency, Patman paper, or tampered valuation—is being passed at Amana since the year-end for the first time in seventy-five years. And rumor has it that a bank, in which the individual colonists may store up the rewards from their industry, is to be the next step.

It has taken all these years in the Iowa prairie to prove to the Amana people that the common sharing of essential value—regardless of the hours tilled in the vineyard—is a failure. The leaders of this staunch folk are deserving of congratulation for being open-minded about the philosophy they had nurtured so long. The Community of the True Inspiration now has some economic inspiration to extend to its fellow settlers of the Middle West countryside—the Farmers' Union, for example, and the Farmers' Holiday Association.

Communism Ends for Cows as Well as Folk at Amana

Cedar Rapids Gazette, January 22, 1933

Even the cows are denied the advantages of communism since the Amana Colonies adopted the capitalistic system. The free and easy days of browsing and ruminative cud chewing with no thought of productive responsibilities are over.

Muley and Bossie must be "worth their groceries" and prove it if they continue to enjoy the privileges of board and room, medical care and valet service afforded at the colony barns....recently at Amana while Rudolph Pitz of Middle, and Phillip Geiger, farm manager here, were checking up on the productivity of the individuals in the herd.

Mr. Pitz, who is dairy foreman at Middle, has been delegated by the colony management to direct a herd improvement or cow test association project in each of the seven villages. Once a month, he weighs the milk and takes a sample for butterfat test. When sufficient records are obtained on which to base a conclusion, it is expected that full-balanced grain rations will be fed each cow in ratio to amount of production. The animals which do not return a profit above feed cost will be eliminated. One test already has been made of each cow in the seven herds and the second is in progress. The milking herds total more than 500 head, of which 360 are now in milk....

Drop Communism for Capitalism
Iowa's Old Amana Colonies Abandon Socialistic Scheme

The Panama American, February 12, 1933

The last outpost of communism in the United States has fallen.

At the very time when technocrat and economic prophet unite in funeral orations for the capitalist and price system, that same system swallows up the last important social community experiment in the country.

The seven Amana villages with their 26,000 fertile acres in the valley of the Iowa River, which have maintained their communal life intact for 86 years, have gone over to a democratic capitalism.

Real money jingles in the pockets of the Amana workers for the first time. Time-clocks are punched in the weaving mills, which are humming, and may go on a 24-hour-a-day schedule soon. Meals are being served in family homes rather than in community dining rooms. Already 171 Amana residents own their own homes, a thing never before heard of in the villages. Every resident is a stockholder in the corporation, rather than simply a member of the community. Visions open up before some of the younger members of some day even owning an automobile.

New life throbs through the community which plodded along so quietly for nearly a century. New products are being marketed in an energetic manner. The construction of several automobile service stations in the modern brick-and-concrete style indicates that when new dwellings are erected in the Amana villages, they will be up to the minute. There is scarcely an adult without a job, and these are provided for by store credits charged to the corporation.

All this is no less than a revolution on a small scale. An orderly revolution, and one which has been put in effect over a period of months, but a really revolution for the Amana villages. The stolid, religious Germans who founded them do not change rashly nor quickly. An 86-year-old plan, which had always operated with reasonable success, was carefully studied before change was introduced. Faced by the depression, the community found its long-sustained profits dwindling. The younger people no longer worked for the common good alone, as had their fathers and grandfathers. They either found that they could live on the community without work, or began to want things for themselves as a reward for superior work. No plans were worked out for a community democracy in which each should share according to his service.

The society was capitalized for about $1,500,000, with two kinds of shares, common voting and prior distributive.

Each adult member of the society holds one voting common share of stock. Thus ultimate control is a pure democracy, as each member has one vote regardless of his other interests.

The prior distributive shares are held on the basis of the service rendered the society. The total value of the society's holding was divided by the number of years of service of all the members. That gave the approximate value of one year's service. Thus the older members own the greater part of the prior shares. These shares are to pay 7 percent dividends, and all earnings above this requirement are to be divided pro-rata among the common voting shares.

This essentially democratic arrangement shows the unique compromise that has been reached at Amana between capitalism and communism. Free medical and dental services, care of the aged and the incapacitated, provision for burial, all at the common expense of the corporation, show how the social sense has survived the change to capitalism.

Modern office methods and equipment have been installed, whereas in former days most of the company's business was carried in the heads of the leaders, with the help of a couple of huge ledgers. Even an outside manager has been brought in. Not that there no smart business men in the Amana community. There were plenty. But the manager was brought in because it was felt that his outside contacts and knowledge of up-to-date procedure would be of value. He is Arthur A. Barlow of Cedar Rapids, a man experienced both in banking and industrial procedure.

The payroll system has been adjusted to put it on the basis of pay according to work done. Weavers in the woolen mills, which produce blankets and textiles and are the society's largest and most important industry, have been placed on a piece-work basis which conforms to that used in most mills outside. The workers are paid on a per yard scale, with deductions for flaws in the cloth they turn out. On the farms, production records are being kept to keep check on the efficiency and production of both cows and milkers. Efficient methods aimed at assuring production from every worker are being introduced, and most of the products, especially those of the mills, are being sold as fast as they can be produced. Meats, flour, preserved fruits and various kinds of expert handiwork are being marketed.

One interesting sidelight on the change was that consumption of bread decreased 50 percent since meals began to be served in private, due to elimination of waste in the community kitchens.

In getting the old, vine-covered plank dwelling-houses of the villages out from under common and into private ownership, many of the distributive-preferred shares were turned back to the society by those who wished to exchange them for their own houses.

Externally, the Amana towns are much the same. No paint is to be seen on the dwellings, for the old-fashioned and unyielding religious belief of these Hessians called a painted house a "worldly vanity." No movies or shows of any kind have been permitted, and the old faith of Amana is a stern ascetic business.

Undoubtedly the religious zeal in which the Amana community was founded supplied the motive power that kept it alive for so many years. That zeal is fading in the younger generation, and it is they who insisted on the quiet "revolution" which has now taken place.

Thus Amana, largest and richest of surviving American experiments in communism, goes the way of Oneida, Harmony, Icaria, Zoar and Brook Farm, all conceived in a lofty idealism, and all wrecked on the reefs of human frailty.

Photograph by William Noe

Religion Remains Unchanged Today In Amana Colonies

The Times, Davenport, Iowa, June 10, 1933
By Daryl James Jones

While their industrial life is being reorganized to meet the needs of 20th century competition, residents of once communistic Amana have retained unchanged their religion which had its beginnings more than 200 years ago.

Church and government have been separated in the new corporation, but the church directors conduct their religious services as before. Each Sunday, residents, clinging on that day to the picturesque calicos and sackcloth suits, go to the meetinghouse where the simple service is read.

The very foundations of Amana are based on their religious ideals which arose in Hease, Germany. Leaders of their sect were believed to have the power of direct inspirations from the Almighty.

Persecution in Europe led the colonists first to Ebenezer, New York, in 1842. They came in 1854 to Iowa and purchased 3,000 acres of fertile soil.

Own 30,000 Acres

As they prospered, more land was added, until the colonists now own 30,000 acres of the richest soil in the Hawkeye state.

Mrs. Bertha M. Shambaugh, in her recent book, *Amana That Was and Amana That Is,* describes an Amana Sabbath. The book is published by the State Historical Association of Iowa.

"The gay pinks and blues and lavenders and tans of the growing up girls, of Amana that is, are for the hour laid aside," she writes, "and 'Sisters All,' young and old, in the orthodox costume of 200 years and more ago, with shoulder and shawl and severe black cap, slip quietly through the side streets and inner paths to their own entrance to the church. And 'Brothers All,' young and old, less orthodox in dress, enter quietly at the other end of the long stone building. Held firmly in the right arm of each Brother and Sister is the *Psalter-Spiel of Rock and Gruber* and the *Bible of Moses and Paul.*"

Service is Simple

"There is a silent prayer. The presiding elder announces a hymn. A tenor among the Brothers sounds the first note; a high soprano among the Sisters takes it up, and the congregation unite in the austere, metrical chant of the non-conformist of three centuries ago.

"Bibles are drawn from their pasteboard cases. The presiding elder announces the fifty-eighth chapter of Isaiah, which is read verse by verse by the elders and the congregation. There is a rythmic rustle as the bibles are slipped into their cases and the congregation arises to sing a closing hymn.

"The presiding elder pronounces a benediction, and the congregation responds with an Amen.

"As quietly as they came, the people leave the church—the women by one exit, the men by another."

Photograph of the Amana Church by Fred Kent

The Amana Colony Keeps Picturesque Charm Despite the "Great Decision"

Kansas City Times, May 6, 1933

It has now been almost two years since the members of the Amana Society made their "great decision" to abandon their constitution as a religious corporation under the laws of the state of Iowa, with the provision that all property should be held by them in common, and to reorganize under some other system which would permit the individual ownership of that property. But although the new scheme of organization, involving several radical alterations in the social and economic life of their remarkable community, has been in effect about a year, the casual visitor who returns to the Amanas fearing they may have lost something of their peculiar charm in the change, will be happily relieved.

In outward appearance, at least, the seven Amana villages still give the impression of having been transplanted bodily from another part of the world. It usually is said they resemble so many German villages, tucked away in their pleasant little valley of southeastern Iowa. But despite the fact that many of the inhabitants are of German origin and the German language still is widely spoken among them, it might be hard to find an architectural counterpart in Germany for Amana or any of the other villages that lie around it.

The fact is that although the Amanas appear foreign, they are really like nothing so much as themselves.

Amanas See Success in Their Own "New Deal"

Colonists Say They're Better Off Under Planned Economy
Hope for Better Days as Industries Hold Their Own

Des Moines Register, October 22, 1933

How successful has the Amana colony been under its planned capitalistic economy set up a little more than a year ago? The Sunday Register *sent a staff writer to the Amanas last week to find the answer to that question. His story follows.*

One young man of Amana, Saturday, voiced the lament of his generation, and neither communism nor capitalism has led him into the promised land. "Yesterday," he said, "I worked 10 hours. Every day is like that. Last month I made $30. I have a wife and home of my own. I have a car. I want more education. I want enough money to buy my groceries, clothe my family, pay my taxes—enough to live decently. I want justice...liberty...opportunity..."

The ruddy glow of Teutonic ancestry was in his cheeks and the same ancestry gave him the hereditary privilege of membership in the Amana Society, but life and youth have left him with yawning chasms of dissatisfaction.

June 1, 1932, the long heralded and much explained "change" took place in the Amana colonies—those seven villages strewn along 26,000 acres of land in the Iowa River valley. From a communistic social setup, which had endured for more than four generations, we were told, the colonies were to change overnight into a capitalistic society. Some cited the long endurance of the social scheme employed in the colonies as proof of the workability of communism. Others pointed to the ultimate "change" as proof that communism, despite the Soviets, was essentially a bad doctrine.

A few remembered that the 1,500 members of the Amana colonies were no particles of matter in the test tube of experiment, but human beings engaged in the quite ordinary occupation of seeking happiness.

Originally, a devoted band of True Inspirationalists turned over their temporal affairs to the church elders as the simplest disposition of earthly cares in order that the main purposes—which were spiritual purposes—might better be served. Unified by a tradition of persecution and a religious spirit embodied in the name "Amana"—remain true—the zealots shared both the labor of living and the fruits of that labor in communal brotherhood.

Since 1843, however, both the temper of the people and the conditions of life have changed. In 1932, that change was culminated in the "new deal" of the Amanas. Under that "new deal," the communism, which the majority of the people believed was outworn, was changed to managed economy in which individual initiative—"rugged individualism"—was spurred by the revival of job competition and by the payment of material rewards in approximate ratio to ambition and ability. The church and the economy of the colonies were definitely separated.

Prophet of the "new deal" in the Amana colonies is Arthur Barlow, who is not a member of the community of the True Inspiration, but a Cedar Rapids, Iowa, businessman and regular attendant at Rotary Club luncheons. Barlow is business manager of the colony enterprises under the reorganization, and with the tactics of an outer world, he is attempting to put those enterprises on a "paying basis."

According to Rotary standards, the success of the new manager probably has not been startling. Barlow himself declines to offer figures as to the solvency of the woolen mills, the farming industries, the many stores and shops of the seven villages of the Amanas.

Leaders of the colonies within their ranks, however, declare the industries are "holding their own" at the present time and hope for better days to come when the pall of the international depression lifts.

By colony standards, however, the success of the new manager has been quite satisfactory. Virtually without dissent the colony members agree the efficiency of their economy has been immeasurably increased and that they are "better off" under the reorganization plan.

Barlow also declines to offer figures as to the salaries paid by the industries, and members of the colony are extremely reticent to discuss the question.

From conversations with numerous members, however, it was learned that the salaries range from 10 cents an hour up. How far up they go it is impossible to say. Barlow was hired at a salary of $5,000 a year for half-time work at the colony. Mornings he is a Cedar Rapids businessman, and afternoons, he is business manager of the colonies. His probably is the highest salary.

It is pointed out that in addition to the money salaries, members of the colonies are stockholders in the enterprise; that they receive some merchandise at a discount; that practically all members own their own homes and have them unencumbered; that they have good-sized lots with large gardens; that wood is available for fuel at a very nominal rate; that they receive medical and dental care free; that they are financially secure against illness, accident or old age, and that they have free burial. If this is less actual security than the old economy afforded, nearly all the members of the colony believe the new economy's added liberty more than compensates [for] the difference.

Outwardly the colonies have changed since June 1, 1932. Paint is being applied to some of the houses which have not known that protection since they were built nearly a century ago. Three modern filling stations—the pride of Manager Barlow—have been erected to bid for tourist trade, and new road signs advertising colony industries have been erected on nearby highways.

Many homes have known modern plumbing for the first time this year and more automobiles are being owned by colony members. More colony members are visiting the outside world and radios and furnaces are appearing in the homes.

Colony youths and girls are attending high school, and many dream of college. Formerly only colony members chosen for professional services in the colony were afforded education above the eighth grade unless they could provide it themselves.

Community kitchens and dining halls, where formerly colony members dined together, are being converted to other uses since meals are taken in the individual homes. One kitchen has been converted to a modern physician's office; another is a tearoom for tourists, and others are now enlarged dwelling quarters.

Timber, which covered nearly half of the 26,000 acres of land, is being cleared and the land will be tilled to increase the agricultural efficiency....change was in progress long before the advent of the reorganization.

"The first generation," said the Amana druggist, a philosopher, "has an idea and lives for that idea. The second generation perpetuates that idea for the sake of their fathers, but their hearts are not in it. The third generation openly rebels against the task of mere perpetuation of institutions founded by their grandfathers—it is always the same...."

Paved roads, radio, telephone, newspapers and the automobiles combined to shatter that lovely isolation from the world and from worldly strife which the founders had envisioned. Tourists, sightseers and antique hunters flocked to the quaint old-worldliness of the colonies with their unpainted wooden houses and their houses of old stone and old brick and the moss-lined canal.

Young colonists traveled away from the mother Amana. Some sought education; others sought adventure; some sought money. The singleness of religious purpose waned with the succeeding generations and the economy which was founded on that singleness of purpose inevitably was destined to change.

"It happened outside the colony," said Gus Miller, president of the Amana Church Society, "and it happened in Amana. The church ceased to become all-important, and material things entered in more and more."

When that happened the church-imposed restraint and the church-imposed economy became merely irksome. With the spiritual influence of the church, four generations of communal life and a hardy German stock in the background, the people of the seven villages of Amana, however, have preserved a spiritual integrity which is evident in their daily life....

If their former mode of life was worn threadbare, they now seek to give it new content. If their thoughts have turned to material things, they have not forgotten the spiritual value of material things.

"We have divorced the church from our economy," said Dr. C.F. Noe, physician of Amana, whose educational experience includes both the University of Iowa and the University of Berlin, "and no longer will we tolerate those who have sought economic advantage by feigning religious belief. We have driven the money-changers out of the temple," said Dr. Noe.

Thus the young man of Amana and all the people of the seven villages of the Amanas are attempting to meet the complexities of an imperfect world.

Amanas Ask Federal Aid on Lighting

Des Moines Register, October 24, 1935

AMES, IA—The Amana Society, located in Iowa county, is the most recent applicant for federal funds to be used for rural electrification, Frank D. Paine, rural electrification engineer, announced here Wednesday.

The society plans to construct 11.9 miles of line and has applied for a grant of $34,500, Paine said.

Furnish Other Services

The society owns 25,000 acres of land, divided into seven small villages and several extensive farms. In June, 1932, the Amanas were reorganized from a communistic society into a co-operative stock company.

The society, which also furnishes free medical, hospital and dental attention, free burial and undertaker's services, and care in old age and invalidism when necessary, is also under contract with its members to furnish, if at all possible, continuous employment.

Will Purchase Power

The society wishes, in so far as possible, to employ its own members as laborers on the electrification project. The society plans to purchase its power at wholesale rates from the Iowa Electric Light & Power Co. and has estimated its total annual consumption at 583,500 kilowatt hours.

Electrification, Pain reported, is now limited in the Amana colony to the power load in the woolen mills, wood working mills and a few scattered farm lighting systems. A poll of the colony, however, has revealed that members of the society, 95 percent of whom own their own homes, will welcome the opportunity to obtain electricity, Paine stated.

First Amana High School Opens to Mark One More Step in Colony Modernization

Communistic Education Ended with Eighth Grade; Corporation Adds 2 More Years with Activity Program

Cedar Rapids Gazette, Fall 1934

High school bells this week will sound another note in the colony transition from communism to corporation. With the introduction of a superintendent of schools and a two-year high school, the Amanans will become still more like their neighbors from whom they have lived apart for so many years.

Like all other transformations in the Amanas, this change has been taking place gradually, beginning with the modernizing of the traditional social customs when the younger generation began to take over the reins. Before the advent of this quiet revolution, only a few destined to become the doctors, dentists, pharmacists and teachers in the colonies, were educated above the eighth grade. Last year some thirty Amana boys and girls were enrolled at Marengo and Williamsburg high schools. This week, under the superintendence of John R. Nevelin of Manly, the first Amana high school will open.

Since Amana, as a school district, has been paying tuition for students going to Marengo or Williamsburg, the change will involve little or no financing problem. Three upstairs rooms in a two-story brick building are available at Middle Amana to house ninth and tenth grade classes, whose members now constitute the bulk of the high school enrollment away from home. If the experiment succeeds, eleventh and twelfth grades may be added.

......

Some colonists who completed their education, when only an eight-year school course was offered in the Amanas, are enrolled in the new high school as part-time students. Commercial subjects and German are especially popular among these graduates....

187

It Was Forbidden at Amana

Rules or No Rules, Bill Zuber Learned How to Play Baseball

When Laws Changed: He Really Started to Work

Des Moines Register, September, 1935

Bill Zuber, 1944
New York Yankees

Probably no big leaguer of today had scantier opportunity for early baseball training, for steeping himself in the tradition and lore of the game, than did William Henry (Bill) Zuber, one-third of Iowa's contribution to the Cleveland Indians. For Zuber, 23-year-old righthand pitcher, is a product of the state's Amana colonies where, in his formative years, baseball, even throwing or any type of play with a ball, was expressly forbidden.

All Shared Alike

The situation is different in the Amana colonies now. But when Bill was a boy, children were taught industry—the serious side of life—almost exclusively. Games and other such "time-wasters" were excluded from their lives.

The colony government was communistic. Rigid rules and disciplinary measures were designed by the elders who had led their followers west from New York to settle in the Mississippi valley near Iowa City. Work and benefits were shared alike. When a boy finished grammar school at 13 or 14, he was apprenticed to learn a useful trade or was put to work in one of the colonies' various enterprises.

Young Zuber became a farm laborer at the Middle Amana colony. His father, William C. Zuber, has been the colony farm manager for 27 years. All his life, except during recent baseball seasons, Bill has lived in a huge red brick house of old Amana style across from the rows of barns where the colonists' purebred hogs and cattle are kept. As is the Amana custom, the house is divided into several apartments and many of the relatives also live there. Occupying one of the apartments are his sister and her husband who also is named William Henry Zuber. However, the brothers-in-law are not related.

Bill Zuber was as far removed from a sports environment as an Iowa boy could be. Yet baseball always had a strong attraction....

Didn't See Games

"Bill always managed to play ball in spite of rules," says his father. "He had a ball to play with, even if it was one made of wound string. I'll have to confess that I bought him a real baseball when he was a little older, although the game was forbidden even on weekdays. He was always begging me and his sisters to throw the ball to him—high over the house—so he could catch it. He always caught it, too.

"I don't know how he became so interested in baseball. We had no teams and he didn't see games outside. He just loved to throw a ball and catch it. Born in him, I guess."

Enforcement of rules against baseball became lax a few years before reorganization of the colony government let down the bars to sports and colony teams were organized. Young Zuber pitched for the Middle Amana club. His record there earned him a position with a team in a Cedar Rapids, Ia. semi-pro league.....he was farmed out successively to Fargo, N.D.; Zanesville, Ohio, and Milwaukee, Wis.

It is a tradition in the Amanas that a colonist may leave but he always returns. Zuber is no exception. There are no winter trips to semi-tropical climes for him. When the baseball season ends, he heads straight for home. In the Amanas he is still a "farm worker," merely on leave of absence for the duration of the baseball season.

Runs a Tractor

"Bill never rests for more than three days after he returns home," the senior Zuber says. "Then he runs a tractor in the field and helps with the cattle and hogs. He likes that, too. He was very homesick when he first went away to play ball, but he got over that, of course. I don't think, though, that he will ever leave Amana for good."

The Cleveland rookie's mother thinks, too, that her boy will "settle down" in the colonies. She believes he will someday marry and live in one of Amana's picturesque old houses. "There's a girl in the colony that he doesn't forget," she explains. "Yes, I think Amana will always be my boy's real home."

Epilogue

The Amana Heritage Society

The Amana Heritage Society is a non-profit membership-supported organization incorporated in 1968, whose purpose is to collect, preserve and interpret the buildings, artifacts and documents which comprise the cultural heritage of the Amana Colonies. The Amana Heritage Society operates four historical sites in the Colonies to preserve Amana's heritage for the community and tell its story to visitors.

The Museum of Amana History in the village of Amana is the primary museum site. The museum has been actively collecting artifacts since its inception and continues to receive donations from the community. Comprised of three 19th century buildings set in spacious grounds, the museum gives the visitor a broad overview of Amana's history. Exhibits in the Noé House (built in 1864) trace the history and development of Amana from its German religious origins to the present. Artifacts include furniture, textiles, household furnishings and many examples of the products of communal era crafts and trades. The Schoolhouse (built in 1870) contains the Library and Archives which make the documentary heritage of the Amana Colonies available to researchers. In addition to historical sources, the library collects contemporary newspaper and magazine stories on Amana, as well as research papers, journal articles and dissertations. An audio-video presentation on Amana history is shown regularly in the Schoolhouse auditorium. The Schoolhouse is also the site of the Museum Shop which offers a wide selection of books, toys, and crafts. The original washhouse/woodshed, an integral part of communal Amana, contains gardening and wine-making displays.

The Communal Kitchen and Coopershop Museum in Middle Amana is the only remaining intact communal kitchen in the Amana Colonies. The visitor can see the original brick hearth, wooden dry sink and tubs, and kitchen tools which served to feed the community. In the adjoining dining room, long tables are set with china and silver.

A guide tells the visitor about the daily routine of the women who worked in the communal kitchens. The Coopershop is adjacent to the kitchen. Built in 1863, it served the domestic, agricultural and industrial sectors of the community by providing a variety of barrels, tubs, and containers.

The Community Church Museum in Homestead is one of seven Amana village churches of the Community of True Inspiration. Built in 1865 from local brick, the building is much as it was 100 years ago. Hosts guide the visitor through the church, explaining the religious background and foundation of Amana from the 18th century to the present day.

The Communal Agriculture Museum housed in one of South Amana's oldest barns has an unusual collection of implements and machinery which, assisted by photographs and texts, tell the story of farming in communal Amana. The barn itself is a wonderful example of the builder's craft, with its beams hewn from native timber and mortise and tenon joints.

Society Leadership

The Amana Heritage Society is a leader in the historic preservation of the Amana Colonies. It sponsors educational workshops, provides information on historic properties and offers technical assistance for preservation projects in the community.

The museums and programs of the Amana Heritage Society continue to be guided by its original mission statement and the directive of Christian Metz (1794-1867) to "Let your heritage not be lost, but bequeath it as a memory, treasure and blessing." The Society strives to be the historian of the Amana community, expanding its collections of artifacts and documents—and ideas—and making them available to the general public and researchers.

Dates in Communal Amana History

1842   Decision to leave Germany and go to America.

1843-   More than 800 followers came to America, founding the
1846   Ebenezer, N.Y., Colonies.

1854   Committee goes to Kansas; Committee goes to Iowa; in
           December, the site of Amana was selected in Eastern

1856   Iowa. West and South Amana villages sites selected.

1857   High Amana founded.

1859   Amana Society incorporated.

1860   East Amana founded.

1861   Village of Homestead purchased in order to obtain access
           to railroad.

1862   Middle Amana founded.

1867   Christian Metz, leader of the moves to America and to
           Amana, died.

1883   Barbara Heinemann Landmann, last inspired leader, died.

1932   Amana Society reorganized as a commercial, tax-paying
           corporation.

1932   Amana Church Society organized as non-profit
           organization.